101 Ways You Can Help Save the Planet Before You're 12!

101 Ways You Can Help Save the Planet Before You're 12!

Joanne O'Sullivan

LARK BOOKS

A Division of Sterling Publishing Co. Inc.
New York / London

Editor:
Joe Rhatigan &
Rain Newcomb

**Art Director &
Photo Researcher:**
Ginger Graziano

Cover Designer:
Celia Naranjo

Cover Photograph:
Steve Mann

Library of Congress Cataloging-in-Publication Data

O'Sullivan, Joanne.
  101 ways you can help save the planet before you're 12! / Joanne
O'Sullivan. -- 1st ed.
      p. cm.
  Includes bibliographical references and index.
  ISBN 978-1-57990-861-4 (pbk. : alk. paper)
  1. Environmental protection--Citizen participation--Juvenile literature.
I. Title. II. Title: One hundred and one ways you can help save the planet
before you're 12!
  TD171.7.O88 2009
  640--dc22

                         2008034578

10 9 8 7 6 5 4 3 2 1

First Edition

Published by Lark Books, A Division of
Sterling Publishing Co., Inc.
387 Park Avenue South, New York, NY 10016

Text © 2009, Joanne O'Sullivan
Photography © 2009, Lark Books unless otherwise specified
Illustrations © 2009, Lark Books unless otherwise specified

Photography credits are found on page 142 and constitute an extension of this copyright page.

Distributed in Canada by Sterling Publishing,
c/o Canadian Manda Group, 165 Dufferin Street
Toronto, Ontario, Canada M6K 3H6

Distributed in the United Kingdom by GMC Distribution Services,
Castle Place, 166 High Street, Lewes, East Sussex, England BN7 1XU

Distributed in Australia by Capricorn Link (Australia) Pty Ltd.,
P.O. Box 704, Windsor, NSW 2756 Australia

If you have questions or comments about this book, please contact:
Lark Books, 67 Broadway, Asheville, NC 28801, 828-253-0467

Manufactured in China
All rights reserved
ISBN 13: 978-1-57990-861-4

For information about custom editions, special sales, and premium and corporate purchases, please contact
Sterling Special Sales Department at 800-805-5489 or specialsales@sterlingpub.com.

Contents

Introduction

Spider-Man can crawl on ceilings. Wonder Woman can deflect a bullet with the flick of her wrist. These superpowers are nothing compared with what you can do—you can help save the planet.

You don't need a cape or a tricked-out car to do it. You just need passion, commitment, and some great ideas, such as the ones you'll find in this book. Imagine being able to reverse the environmental damage caused by hundreds of pollution-spewing cars. You can do it simply by changing the light bulbs in your house. Visualize a world where endangered animals can thrive again. You can help make it real by spreading the word and making your opinions known.

Clean up streams, increase recycling, decrease waste—you can do it all and still be on time for dinner. Isn't that a powerful feeling?

Just like a superhero, you will find that once you've tapped into your power to help the Earth, you'll always find new ways to use it: at home, at school, in your neighborhood, or in the larger community. Sometimes you'll see quick results and sometimes you won't. But even if you can't see the impact of what you're doing, it's there and you are making a difference.

No matter your age or where you live, your planet needs super you. Are you ready to answer the call?

How to Use This Book

Start by reading the first two entries. They might help you understand better how to begin. Then, look through the list and figure out which things you and your family might already be doing, and which things will be next on your list. Remember, you don't have to do everything in this book. Start some new projects and see them through, or just develop some good new habits. Map out your activities for the upcoming months so that they coincide with the seasons. And don't forget to celebrate! You'll find out that there are more "Earth holidays" than you might have known about, and each one represents an opportunity to learn and to spread the word about an issue that's important to our planet's health.

Also, get your family, teachers, and classmates involved. The great anthropologist Margaret Mead once said, "Never underestimate the power of a small group of committed citizens to change the world. Indeed, it has never been done otherwise."

Finally, share this book and what you learn from it with friends. Recycling is one of the best ways a kid can help the planet, and pre-used ideas work just as well for one kid as for the next!

A superhero's work is never done. There could be more than 101 (1001?!) ways you can be a better citizen of Planet Earth. Use your super-strong will and determination to come up with ways to help the Earth that today's grownups have never thought of!

One of the great things about our planet is its variety—so many different kinds of plants and animals, places, and ways to live. People come in lots of different types, too, and that keeps things interesting. When it comes to helping the planet, everyone has something to offer. What about you? Think about what gets you really excited and how you can put your energy and enthusiasm to use for a good cause. Do you love animals? Join a group that helps protect endangered species. Are you a natural-born leader? Get others excited about helping the environment. Check this list to find your eco-type and you're on your way to making a difference.

Nature Kid

Kayaking, rock climbing, camping, hiking, mountain biking—you love to get out in the great outdoors. If being out in nature is your idea of the perfect way to spend the day, you might just be the perfect kid to help preserve those wilderness areas you love so much. Team up with a trail crew and help clear paths so that more people can go hiking, or join a conservation group and learn about what's happening to forests, rivers, and beaches. Nature needs you in order to stay as wonderfully wild as it is.

Eco Activist

Why wait for someone else to take action? You're a doer! If you see a problem, you've just got to jump in and help fix it. If this describes your personality, why not use your leadership skills to help raise awareness about environmental issues or start a group at your school? Come up with a project and recruit helpers. Write letters to your local paper and bring some attention to your issue. If anyone can do it, you can!

Science Fair Star

A new way to harness the power of the sun? An invention made from completely recycled parts? You're on it! The planet needs kids like you to come up with new sources of renewable energy, new ways to be energy efficient, and creative ways to look at the way we live. Use your natural knack for science to help discover how we can protect the planet.

Green Thumb

You can turn a patch of dirt into a thriving garden and make a delicious dinner from it to boot. Use your gift for growing to "plant the seed" about organic growing in the minds of your friends and family. Help show everyone how healthy foods lead to healthier people and a healthier planet.

Creature Teacher

If you could, you'd have a whole zoo full of endangered animals at your house, just so you could protect them. But as it is, you might just have to love your favorite animals from afar. Find out what your favorite species needs, and join groups that help them. Educate your classmates, friends, and family about the threats to different species and how our actions can affect animals thousands of miles away.

Dedicated Do-It-Yourselfer

The thrift store is like a treasure chest for you, and you can't wait to find what marvels await you there. Your passion for finding new life in old things puts you in the perfect position to become a recycling role model. Reuse, reduce, and recycle and watch as others follow your lead.

Still not sure what you're passionate about? Reading this book will definitely give you some ideas.

2 LEARN THE LINGO

As you get more and more involved with green issues, you'll start hearing and reading about all sorts of words and terms that might be unfamiliar to you. Here's a list of terms to get you started.

Biodegradable: Made of mostly organic (natural) material that will naturally decompose over time and be absorbed back into the environment.

Biodiversity: The variety of living things within a certain area or environment or simply the number of different things within those defined areas.

Climate change: A term sometimes used to describe global warming.

Carbon dioxide: A gas that's created by the burning of coal, oil, natural gas, or organic matter. Contributes to greenhouse gases that cause global warming.

Carbon monoxide: A toxic gas produced by the production of fossil fuels.

Carbon neutral: Describes a state of balance between carbon emissions created and those "offset" by activities that remove carbon from the atmosphere, such as planting trees or using clean, alternative energy.

Carbon footprint: An idea used to help people understand the impact that their actions have on the environment. A carbon footprint is usually represented by an amount of CO_2 measured in pounds or tons. For example, if a person's activities create 10 tons of carbon per year, that person's carbon footprint would be expressed as 10 tons.

Carbon offset: A way of decreasing the impact of the greenhouse gases you create. An offset can be something that's purchased, or it can be created by an action, such as planting trees.

Compact fluorescent: A kind of energy-efficient light bulb.

Composting: The decomposition of organic material.

Ecosystem: An interconnected group of living things.

Energy efficient: Uses less electricity, gas, or other fuel than usual in order to function at typical levels.

Energy Star: A standard created by the U.S. government to measure energy efficiency in appliances (such as refrigerators, ovens, and stoves), office equipment, lighting, home

electronics, and heating and cooling systems. An Energy Star label means that the device/product has met or surpassed the government standard.

Fossil fuels: A source of fuel that is formed in the Earth's crust. Some fossil fuels include petroleum, coal, and natural gas.

Global warming: Describes an increase in the "near surface temperature" of the Earth, generally believed by scientists to be caused by higher levels of greenhouse gases (see definition below).

Greenhouse gases: Carbon dioxide, nitrous oxide, methane, ground level ozone, and chlorofluorocarbons are examples of greenhouse gases. They exist naturally to reduce the loss of heat in the Earth's

Habitat: Sometimes used in the same way as ecosystem (see page 11). Describes the environment (consisting of food, shelter, etc.) that a living organism needs in order to survive.

Invasive species: A type of plant or animal that is not native to the area in which it is living. An invasive species can be harmful to native species. The photo to the left shows kudzu, a Japanese plant that's "invading" the southern U.S.

Native species: A type of animal or plant that has existed in a place for a very long time and has become compatible with an ecosystem, working with it instead of against it.

Organic food or products: There are different definitions, but generally, organic food or products are those that are created without the use of pesticides, chemical fertilizers, or artificial additives.

atmosphere, keeping the planet's temperatures compatible with living things. Burning fossil fuels and other industrial processes create more greenhouse gases in addition to those that exist naturally. This raises the temperature of the air in the part of the atmosphere closest to the Earth, contributing to global warming (see page 11).

Ozone: A gas found naturally in the Earth's upper atmosphere. It can also be formed in the lower atmosphere by a chemical reaction created by the presence of polluting gases. This kind of ozone is called ground-level or bad ozone.

Passive solar: Using the energy of the sun without a special device or mechanism. Keeping curtains open to warm a house is one example of a passive solar technique.

Petroleum: A flammable liquid found in the Earth's crust. It's a fossil fuel that can be made into gasoline, oil, and many other fuels. It can also be used to create materials, such as plastics, tar, or wax.

Post-consumer content: Refers to the part of a product, container, or type of packaging that comes from sources that have been recycled or recovered after consumers have used them.

Recycled content: Refers to the part of a product, container, or type of packaging that comes from material that would have otherwise been thrown away.

Renewable energy: Energy that comes from sources that will never be exhausted, such as the wind or sunlight. Fossil fuels are not renewable: eventually the supply of these fuels will be used up.

Toxic: Harmful to living things. The term toxic is also often used to describe harmful chemicals.

Vermicompost: Composting with worms.

Watershed: Describes a geographic area in which all the water drains into a common source, such as a river, stream, lake, or the ocean.

Xeriscaping: Landscaping with plants that don't need watering outside of the natural occurrence of rainfall.

3 Be a Vampire Hunter

Put down the garlic necklace and stop carving the wooden stakes. The vampires you'll be hunting are *energy* vampires that suck resources out of your home. They do it secretly, day and night, without you even knowing it. How can you spot these vampires? They look suspiciously like ordinary household objects—TVs, computers, printers, even your beloved video game console. After you turn them off, many of these electric-powered devices go into "standby" mode. So, even though they look "off," they're actually still sucking power. For example, if you leave your computer plugged in and have a screen saver running, you're really not saving any-thing—your computer is sucking lots of power. Pull the plug on these power vampires when they're not in use. Use a power strip so you can cut the power to several devices at once. If your family is buying a new gadget, find out if it uses standby power. (Energy-efficient models will have a label to distinguish them.) Hunting energy vampires is a lot safer than chasing the blood-sucking kind, and you'll help your family save money and resources. And you won't have to worry about that yucky garlic smell.

4

FILL 'ER UP

When you were younger, did you ever have a raggedy old blanket or stuffed animal that you absolutely couldn't go anywhere without? You probably left it behind years ago, but you might want to consider getting a new, slightly less cuddly constant companion—how about a can't-leave-home-without-it, always-by-your-side water bottle? It may not provide you with exactly the same feeling as your old blanket, but it's still good to have along with you. Here's why: 17 million barrels of oil are used each year just to produce all the disposable plastic water bottles used in the U.S. What's more, only about 12% of disposable water bottles are actually recycled. That means 88% of water bottles end up taking up space in a landfill or becoming litter. When you use a refillable glass, stainless-steel, or ceramic container, you can save money and still enjoy the perfectly safe and refreshing water offered just about every place you go. Plus, you'll be helping to cut back on unnecessary waste. Isn't that a comforting thought?

BY THE WAY, there's no evidence that drinking bottled water is any safer than drinking filtered tap water. In fact, some bottled water IS tap water!

5 Green Your Pet

Don't forget about your pets when working on decreasing your impact on the Earth. There are a lot of simple things you can do to make your pet's paw print a little lighter on the planet.

If you have a dog, there's one thing you must do: pick up the poo. Dog waste can get into waterways and contaminate it. Carry a biodegradable bag when you go for a walk and make a deposit in it when your pooch does the doo.

If you have a cat, choose your litter material carefully. Many people use clumping clay litter because it's easy to clean. Unfortunately, the clay has to be mined, which is not good for the Earth. Also, it's not good for your cat's insides. Use litter made from recycled newspaper, crushed walnut shells, sawdust, wheat, and even corn.

Have your pet spayed or neutered so that he or she doesn't create more little paw prints—pet overpopulation is a big problem for the planet because there aren't enough people who want to take care of all of them.

When your pet's toys wear out, purchase recycled and environmentally friendly replacements.

If you don't have a pet and want one, get one from a shelter—loving an orphaned animal is good for you, your pet, and the planet.

Consider feeding your pet natural and organic pet foods. Check the food packaging to make sure the meat in the food you choose is raised in a sustainable and humane way, without drugs or hormones, and that the meat has been minimally processed. Your pet will thank you with years of better health.

6 Host a Habitat

While you may hear about rain forest and wilderness habitats more often, your very own backyard is a habitat, too. Right now, it may just be home to bugs, but with a little effort you can make it a protected place for a variety of animals. How? Give them what they want—food, water, shelter—and they're sure to come around. Convince your parents to plant shrubs and tall grasses where animals can nest, and fruit trees and berry bushes where they can forage for food. (For best results, research and use native plants. See page 80 for more information.) A birdbath full of clean water will attract birds, and a water feature, such as a pond is sure to lure turtles and frogs. If your backyard is a balcony or even a window box, you can still attract butterflies or hummingbirds by planting flowers that they like, such as zinnias and marigolds. Once you've made your garden more animal-friendly, you can actually apply to have it certified as a National Wildlife Foundation Certified Backyard Wildlife Habitat. It's a great way to *create* habitat when so many of them in this world are being destroyed.

Get more information at www.nwf.org/backyard.

I Empty Your Mailbox

Getting a letter or package in the mail is a wonderful surprise. But when you open your mailbox these days, you often find it filled with junk: catalogs that your family didn't ask for and doesn't want, advertisements, offers for this service or that. Studies show that each person in the U.S. and Canada will receive more than 500 pieces of junk mail this year. And almost half of that is never even opened. But junk mail is more than annoying: it's devastating to forests. Each year, it takes 100 million trees to make those throw-away catalogs and letters. Recycling that junk mail helps, but stopping it from coming in the first place would be even better. There are many web sites that show you how to remove your family's name from all those junk-mail lists. You can even pay an organization to do it for you.

For more informtion, go to www.forestethics.org

While you're at it, convince your parents to pay their bills online and tell the companies to stop sending paper bills.

Spot a Greenwash

More and more people want to live green and that's great! For companies, a greener product can mean an edge over competitors, so many work to make their product in a cleaner, more environmentally sound way. But some companies want to get the credit *without* doing the work. That's called *greenwashing*. Sometimes it can be hard to tell which products are really trying to improve the environment and which are pretending. One way to tell is to read the labels. But what are you looking for? Here are some tips to help you sort out the hoopla from the real deal.

METHYL

nature

Contains natural flavoring!

WHAT IT SAYS	WHAT IT MEANS
Contains natural flavoring	Contains a product which imitates a natural flavor, but is not the actual natural item (corn made in a lab, for example rather than actual corn)
No artificial preservatives	There are artificial additives instead of preservatives
Earth smart	It doesn't really mean anything
Biocompatible	It doesn't mean anything
Environmentally Friendly	It implies that it's good for the Earth, but there's no way to prove it
No additives	This means there really are no artificial ingredients

Green or Greenwash?

Don't be fooled by just a name. Just because a product has a title that starts with "Earth," "Nature," or "Planet," doesn't mean it's green. Always read the label or ingredients.

Just because a product has a picture of a farm, a field of wheat, or a rain forest on the outside, doesn't mean it's environmentally friendly. Again, it's the list of ingredients that will tell you what you need to know.

Look for specifics: "organic," "sustainably harvested," "fair trade," "post-consumer." If the list of ingredients includes lots of 10-letter words that start with "nitro" or end in "methyl" or "ethyl," it's not all natural!

If the company is in business solely to do something that's bad for the environment—say, mine coal or cut-down old-growth trees—whatever they claim to be doing greener doesn't outweigh the harm they do by existing in the first place.

A few green products don't make up for a lot of un-green ones. For example, a car company that sells mostly SUVs promoting their hybrid line or an oil company that destroys animal habitats promoting their "clean" fuel.

Look for products that are certified by an outside organization. That means they can back up their claims.

9 MAKE IT LAST

The old saying "Waste not, want not" means that if you're careful with what you've got, you'll always have enough. This is true for us as individuals and families and for the planet—if we use our resources wisely and carefully, there's plenty to go around. Try looking at what you've got in a new way with the goal of not wasting. Is there still a little more toothpaste in that tube? Instead of throwing it out, cut the top off so you can squeeze some more toothpaste out of the tube. Wash out your plastic sandwich bag (if you use one—see page 36) and use it again.

Here are some more ideas you can use:

FOOD
✔ Have a creative leftover night. Issue a challenge: who can make the best meal from what you've already got in the fridge and pantry?

If you have some stretching solutions of your own, share them with everyone you know!

CRAYONS

✔ Collect your old, broken crayons and put pieces of them into the holes of a muffin tin. Get an adult to heat the oven to 150°F (66°C). Bake the crayons for about 15 minutes. The wax will melt, and you'll have a whole new, multicolored, round crayon! If you've got soap or candy-making molds, you can make the crayon into different shapes.

SOAP

✔ Don't let it stay wet and dissolve into soap scum.
✔ When you're down to scraps, grate the soap with a cheese grater. Put the scraps into an empty squeeze bottle with a funnel, add water, and you can use it as liquid soap.
✔ Mix liquid or dishwashing soap with water, and then pour it in a larger container. The water doesn't affect its cleaning ability; it just makes it last longer.

PENS

✔ If you have a pen with ink in it that doesn't work, ask a parent to help you apply heat to the end of the pen by holding it close to an iron or other heat source. This should get the ink running again.

SHAMPOO

✔ Most bottles say something like "lather, rinse, repeat." Don't repeat. Your hair will get clean enough the first time, and your shampoo will last longer.

SHOES

✔ Use waterproofing soap on them to protect them from water damage and keep them looking new.
✔ Have them resoled or reheeled instead of throwing them out.
✔ Put baking soda or rolled up newspaper pages (really!) in your shoes to keep them from getting too smelly.

10 / Give a Green Gift

Some of the best gifts in life don't come wrapped up in disposal packaging. In fact, they can't be put into a package at all: they're experiences. Instead of bringing another product into the world, why not celebrate a birthday, Mother's Day, Father's Day, or any other day worth celebrating by giving a memory-making happening instead of a thing? A fishing trip for Dad? A trip to a museum that you can take together? A family pass to a national park? And for the big gift-giving holidays, talk with your family and friends about doing this for each other. Skipping the stuff and spending time together is good for your relationships and good for the planet—your memories will never end up in a landfill!

11 CHILL OUT!

Here's a simple idea that can make a big difference: when you're washing your hands or face, brushing your teeth, rinsing vegetables for dinner, or even washing the dishes, use cold water instead of warm or hot. Make sure your family washes clothes in cold water, too. Why does it matter? If you're like most families, water heating is the third-largest expense in your monthly bill. Your teeth and hands really won't get any cleaner with hot water, and unless your clothes are super dirty, cold water will clean them just as well as hot. Don't worry, you don't have to take a shower in cold water (unless you want to)! But see page 86 for more water efficiency tips.

12 BECOME AN ECO EXPERT

Most people know a little bit about the environment: there's something called global warming and it's bad; recycling is good. But there's an old saying "Knowledge is Power," and if you have knowledge about the planet's problems, you'll discover the power to help solve them. Educate yourself on the issues you care about. Read books, visit web sites, join organizations, subscribe to magazines (online!), see for yourself first hand. Make an effort to actually *memorize* facts about your issue, but don't stop there. Find out about other opinions on the issue, especially those that differ from your own. When it comes to the environment, there's no such thing as too much information.

WEB SITES

The Greens
www.meetthegreens.org

EPA Explorer's Club
www.epa.gov/kids

Kids Planet
www.kidsplanet.org

Kids Do Ecology
www.nceas.ucsb.edu/nceas-web/kids

Planet Slayer
www.abc.net.au/science/planetslayer/

Polar Action Guide
http://www.savebiogems.org/polar/polaraction.pdf

EEK! Environmental Education for Kids
www.dnr.state.wi.us/org/caer/ce/eek

MAGAZINES

National Geographic Kids
http://kids.nationalgeographic.com

Ranger Rick
www.nwf.org/rangerrick

Dolphin Log
www.dolphinlog.org/frm_dolphinLog.html

Zoobooks
www.zoobooks.com

13

CHANGE THE MARGINS!

Could you help save paper with just a couple of clicks? It's worth a try. The next time you're using your computer to write a paper or send a letter, follow these steps.

IF YOU HAVE A MAC:
Go to the "Format" section and scroll down to "Document." Go to "Margins."

IF YOU HAVE A PC:
Go to the "File" section, and scroll down to "Page Setup."

CHECK OUT THE SIZE OF YOUR MARGINS.
Try making them smaller. You could try a narrower margin on the left and a wider one on the right. Or you could make them both smaller.

If you reduce your margins to .75, studies show you'll save 4.75% paper. Not bad for just a few clicks. Think how much paper (and how many trees) you'd save if you got your family, your school, your school system, or even your city to do the same! Write a letter (with small margins!) to those in charge and get them to make the change, too.

Ask your teacher if he will accept single-spaced reports. This could cut your paper consumption in half. Even better, maybe you could email your homework!

14 Adopt a Species

A cute and cuddly panda, a sweet and playful orangutan: no, you won't ever be able to have one as a pet, but you can adopt one for your classroom. Adopting a species means you choose to support organizations that work to keep the animal from danger. You give the organization financial support, and they'll keep you informed about what they're doing. Adopting a species is a great classroom project. Your class can vote on which animal to adopt and come up with fundraising ideas for the adoption fee. If you choose pandas, for example, you could sell panda-shaped cookies or panda-themed artwork that you make yourself. Or make a Chinese dinner for your parents, and then show a presentation on pandas and why you want to help save them. You'll be raising awareness about an endangered animal and helping to protect it at the same time.

To find out how you can adopt a species, go to http://nationalzoo.si.edu/Support/KidsAdopt

15

Eat Organic

THE BEST FOODS TO BUY ORGANIC

Milk Strawberries Apples
Peaches Pears Grapes Spinach

When you hear the word "organic," you probably think "healthy and natural," but do you know what it really means? The technical definition is a little complicated, but it translates to "grown without pesticides or toxins." That means if it's organic, there's minimal risk of harmful chemicals getting into you through your food. But pesticides can harm more than your body—they hurt the environment, too. Chemicals sprayed onto plants can seep into the ground, drift away in the air, or be swept into rivers, and even the ocean, where they can kill plants or animals. So, the more organic food, the safer the planet. Does organic food really taste better? You'll have to try it for yourself to find out!

Every day is the right day to appreciate what an amazing planet we live on, how wonderful it is to share it with so many different forms of life, and to show how much we care about it through our actions. But there are also special days for us to think about specific parts of it: the sky, the oceans, the birds, and even the ozone layer.

Here are a few dates to mark on your calendar. Plan to do something (ideas provided) and spread the word—making an ordinary day special for the planet.

FEBRUARY 2
WORLD WETLANDS DAY
Visit a wetland near you; participate in a wetland clean up; read about wetlands with your class.

MARCH 22
UN WORLD DAY FOR WATER
Spread the word about water awareness (see page 86); make a presentation to your class about water conservation or ask your teacher if you can do a class water project on this day. Installing a school rain barrel would be a great idea (see page 106).

APRIL 22
EARTH DAY
Get up early and watch the sun rise! Take part in a local celebration, or plan one at your school. Organize a park or river clean-up or a walk-to-school day.

LAST FRIDAY IN APRIL
ARBOR DAY
Plant a tree outside your home or school.

ONE WEEK IN APRIL*
NATIONAL DARK SKY WEEK
Turn out the lights and let the stars shine; read about light pollution (see page 126); participate in Earth Hour; go to a planetarium or observatory.

MAY 3
INTERNATIONAL MIGRATORY BIRD DAY
Go birding! Get out your binoculars and head to a wetland or other bird watching spot. Watch the birds go by on their annual migration.

MAY 18
ENDANGERED SPECIES DAY
Plan a school activity around endangered animals (this might be a great time for an Adopt a Species fundraiser [see page 28 for info]).

MAY 22
WORLD BIODIVERSITY DAY
Read about climate change and how it's affecting different species of plants and animals; write a letter to the editor or your elected official about it (see page 112).

JUNE 5*
WORLD ENVIRONMENT DAY
There's a different topic for World Environment Day every year. Check www.unep.org/wed to find out what's happening this year!

JUNE 8
WORLD OCEAN DAY
Participate in a beach clean up; read a book or watch a movie about ocean creatures; volunteer at a marine rescue center; write a letter to the editor about keeping our oceans and their creatures safe.

SEPTEMBER 16
INTERNATIONAL DAY FOR THE PRESERVATION OF THE OZONE LAYER
Plant an ozone garden (see page 48) at your school; plan a class project about ozone awareness; walk to school or ride a bike.

FIRST MONDAY IN OCTOBER
UN WORLD HABITAT DAY
Read about habitats or do a class presentation; write a letter to the editor about endangered habitats.

DECEMBER 11
INTERNATIONAL MOUNTAIN DAY
Go for a hike or bike on a mountain! Read about mountains in your class, or ask your teacher if your class can do a mountain project.

*Dates change from year to year

17 Check It Out

What's the ultimate renewable resource? Library books! You can check them out and renew them as much as you like. They're also better for the planet than the store-bought kind. How so? Each year, around 30 million trees are used to make books sold in the United States alone. That's a lot of trees. But what's worse is that many of those trees come from endangered forests. When the trees are lost, many animals lose their habitat, too. And then, of course, there's the trees' amazing carbon-converting power. When we lose trees, the carbon they usually absorb has nowhere to go but into the atmosphere. Borrowing a book instead of buying your own can save a tree or two, help lower greenhouse gases, and help preserve animal habitats. If the library doesn't have what you need, try renting a book online just like you would with a movie or game. Or exchange a book you no longer want for one you do. You'll save money and trees at the same time.

Rent that book you're after at www.bookswim.com. Or swap books at www.bookcrossing.com or www.paperbackswap.com.

18 GO SOLAR

Feel the power of the sun! It's the strongest, cleanest, most renew-able energy around and it's absolutely free! You can use *passive* solar energy in simple ways around your home: open your curtains and let the sun come in when it's cold. It will bring its warmth and light with it. (And do the opposite when it's hot.) Or you can use gadgets or devices for active solar power. You can buy solar garden lights to illuminate your outdoor pathways at night, and you can even make a solar heater or water heater as a family project. Make a solar oven to give everyone an idea of how solar power works (see next page). Who knows? Maybe one day you'll invent the next great solar technology!

19 Make a Solar Oven

This oven uses only sunlight as fuel and converts it to heat, which in turn cooks the food. You can make it from a variety of materials, but the simplest one might just be something you have in your recycling bin—two empty pizza boxes. (You can find even simpler one-pizza-box ovens online. We like this one because it works well.)

MATERIALS
- 2 pizza boxes, one larger than the other
- Pencil
- Scissors or craft knife
- Aluminum foil
- Newspaper or styrofoam packing
- Nontoxic, black paint
- Paintbrush
- Nontoxic glue
- Sunglasses
- String
- Tape
- Cooking pan
- Clear plastic wrap

What You Do

1. **WARNING:** Treat this solar cooker as a real oven and exercise caution when using it. Center the small pizza box on top of the large one with one side touching (figure 1). Outline all four sides of the smaller pizza box on the lid of the larger box. Set the small box aside and carefully cut out three sides of the square you just drew. Leave the fourth side attached so you still have a connected lid.

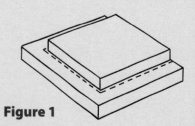

Figure 1

2. Line the inside of the large box with aluminum foil, and then stuff around the sides with newspaper or styrofoam to fill the space (figure 2). This layer of stuffing acts as insulation to help hold in the heat in the oven. Fit the small box into the large box and add more stuffing if needed to fill the space between the two (figure 3).

3. Paint the inside bottom of the small box, and the outside edges of the large box with the black paint. Black absorbs heat and will increase the heat in the oven. Line the rest of the small box with aluminum foil and glue the foil in place.

4. Spread some glue on the bottom side of the

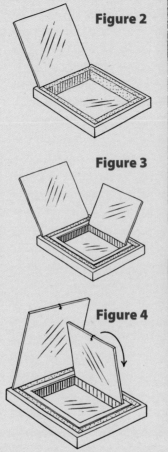

Figure 2

Figure 3

Figure 4

Think about this: If the sun can transform a couple of pizza boxes and some aluminum foil into an oven, just think of the huge possibilities more advanced solar equipment can offer.

two pizza box flaps, and smooth a large piece of aluminum foil on each (shiny side up). Try to keep the foil as wrinkle free as possible.

5. Adjust the flaps so that they reflect light directly into the box when you line the oven up with the sun. Don't look directly at the aluminum and wear sunglasses while you adjust the flaps. Poke a hole in the top of each flap and tie a piece of string through each hole. Tape the other end of each piece of string to the outside of the large box to hold each lid in place at the best angle for reflection (figure 4).

6. Place the food you want to cook on a pan in the oven, and cover the oven with plastic wrap to trap the heat. Select foods that cook at low to medium temperatures. Cookies, biscuits, pizza, nachos, and other simple foods are perfect. It may take 20 minutes to 2 hours for the food to cook depending on what you're making, so plan ahead.

20 · HAVE A LITTERLESS LUNCH

Have you ever checked out the garbage cans in your cafeteria? By the end of lunch period, they're probably overflowing with crumpled up napkins and paper bags, half-eaten sandwiches, and probably a lot of fruit parents sent and kids threw away. Some studies show that each kid more or less throws away his or her weight in lunch garbage every year. But it doesn't have to be that way. With just a few simple changes, you can make a big difference. Carry your lunch in washable, reusable containers, and take along your own reusable fork or spoon instead of the throw-away kind. Use a water bottle instead of disposable juice boxes (see page 15). Pack a cloth napkin every day, and use a lunch box instead of a paper bag. Start a Litterless Lunch Challenge at your school: Take a scale into the cafeteria and have everyone weigh their garbage before they throw it out. Add up the weight. Try to reduce that number over a period of time and see how low you can go.

21 Walk to School Day

Sitting in traffic and listening to the lame radio station your mom chose—there's got to be a better way to start your school day. Talk to your teacher about organizing a Walk to School event to raise awareness about air pollution. Each mile driven in an average car contributes close to a pound of CO_2 (a harmful greenhouse gas) to the atmosphere. When you and other kids from school walk, you're really making a difference. Make your Walk to School day fun. Get everyone to wear a school T-shirt or the school colors. Carry homemade signs so that cars passing by will know why you're walking. Make a "walking school bus" that picks up kids along the way or even a parade. Chances are you'll all have so much fun, you'll want to do it every chance you get.

Schools in every state and province (and even in other countries) are holding Walk to School days. There's even an International Walk to School Day.

Go to www.walktoschool-usa.org to find out which schools in your area participate and to get more ideas on how to make your Walk to School day a success.

22 Do Your Homework First

This may be the planet-saving tip you like the least: do your homework right when you get back from school. While it sounds like a parent favorite, along with "Make Your Bed," "Clean Your Room," and "Don't Bother Your Sister," it's actually a great way to use passive solar energy. The sun is the biggest light source we have, and we get to use it absolutely for free. It's also the cleanest energy source on the planet: It doesn't emit greenhouse gases, and it doesn't release dangerous toxins into the air. So when you do your homework by sunlight, you're actually saving the energy used to operate a light bulb. Still not convinced? Studies show that kids who study by natural light actually get better grades! So throw back the curtains, get to work, and let solar power enhance your brain power.

23 Eat Slow!

What's the opposite of fast food? Slow food! Slow food is food that you can trace back to its source. That means you know exactly where it came from: your garden or the farm down the road, for example. Slow food is the way people *always* ate until fast food was invented in the past century. So, when you eat slow, you're keeping food traditions alive. Slow food is good for your body, good for the planet, and helps you discover how good food can really taste.

Slow Food

Made from scratch

Is produced in the cleanest way possible

All natural

Tastes unique and flavorful

Enjoyed at a table, with friends and family

Is good for you!

Has low environmental impact

Is meant to be enjoyed

Fast Food

Mixed in a big factory

Is made in the cheapest way possible

Full of artificial ingredients

Tastes the same...every time

Eaten in your car

Has little nutritional value

Wastes resources with long distance driving and paper packaging

Is eaten just to eat

For more information about slow food, go to www.slowfoodusa.com.

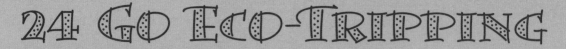

24 Go Eco-Tripping

When your parents start planning the next family vacation, get involved by being the voice for traveling light. Help your family choose a vacation that leaves a more delicate impression on the planet. No matter what your interests are, you can find a vacation that's fun, fulfilling, adventurous, creative, and green. Think about what it is you want to do: see new places, challenge yourself, relax with your family, or learn something new. Then check out some of the tips and ideas on these two pages. Traveling green doesn't have to mean going to a rain forest—going somewhere close to home might even be a better choice. Whatever your destination, travel responsibly (see definition on next page) and enjoy our wonderful planet.

Farm Vacation

Help milk a cow, ride a horse, or harvest grapes. A farm vacation supports local, family-based agriculture, which helps keep economies local (see page 109). Check www.agritourism-world.com

Eco-Tour

An eco-tour generally describes a trip taken to look at nature's wonders: wildlife, rain forests, or coral reefs for example. It's a great way to see first hand what's going on with the environment. Before you decide, though, make sure the trip doesn't do more harm than good. Read reviews from other travelers and ask questions.

Do a Homestay

A homestay is not just a vacation—it's a cultural experience. A family in the location you choose will host you in their home. You'll eat what they eat and learn about their culture first hand. Homestays are great learning experiences, but they're also

OUTDOOR ADVENTURE

Backpacking and camping are great ways to travel green as long as you "tread lightly."

GREEN-UP-YOUR-TRAVEL TIPS

- Travel to a close-by destination to ease your carbon emissions.
- Pledge to travel responsibly: That means trying to improve the conditions of the local environment or people rather than harming them with your presence.
- Bring a reusable water bottle (see page 15 for tips) rather than buying bottled water in each place you go.
- Take the train! It's adventurous and creates fewer emissions than airplane travel. Plus, you're sharing the ride with others and getting to enjoy the view.
- If you have to rent a car, rent a green one.
- Don't leave your energy-friendly habits at home. Turn off your hotel room lights, don't leave the water running, and walk or take public transportation if you can.

good for the planet—sharing resources cuts down on the energy and waste created by hotels. Try www.homestayweb.com for more information.

VOLUNTEER VACATION

Do some good, have some fun. If you want to help out with your time off, clear trails, restore a wetland, plant trees, or work with endangered species. Search online for family volunteer vacations.

ECO-LODGE VACATIONS

Instead of a regular hotel, consider staying in an eco-lodge: a place to stay that was built and operates on green principles: green power, low-waste, and organic and local food. It's a great alternative to a business-as-usual hotel.

25 MAKE YOUR VACATION A STAYCATION

An eco-friendly trip (page 40) is great, but a staycation might be just what your family (and the planet) needs. Instead of traveling somewhere for your spring or fall break, or even in the summer, try staying home and keeping your carbon footprint low. Do those projects that you've been meaning to get to for months. See all those touristy sights that you never get to see in your own town. Sleep late in the morning and stay up late reading in your bed with a flashlight. Unplug the television and computers and play board games like you would if you were at the lake or the beach. You'll give your car and the atmosphere a little break during your break and you'll find out staying home is more fun than you've ever imagined.

Go Retro

Has this ever happened to you? You get to school, all ready to show off your new, happening shirt you got at the mall. You walk into the classroom and there are three kids already there wearing the exact same shirt. How can you avoid this situation? Go Retro. The next time one of your parents takes you shopping for clothes, ask to be taken to the local thrift, consignment, and/or vintage clothes stores. What will you find there? Not just old clothes, but original hippie, grunge, and new-wave clothes you can't find at the mall. It's a closely held fashion designer secret: they actually go to secondhand stores to get ideas for their collections and models love to shop there, too. So, you'll be making a fashion statement by wearing pre-owned clothing as well as a green statement. Buying pre-worn clothes is a great way to decrease consumerism and support recycling.

27 Get Growing

Good relationships are all about give and take. We take a lot from the planet every day—food, energy, shelter, comfort. But how can we give back? Growing a garden is a great place to start. Even if you don't have the space to grow a lot, there are many creative ways to make the planet a little greener. Trees, flowers, vegetables, or berry bushes—plant them from seeds, bulbs, or small plants and watch them grow, bringing color to your life, as well as shelter and food to all kinds of creatures. As a bonus, they'll also help clean the air. If you notice pieces of land in your neighborhood or school grounds that are just dirt, ask if you can plant something there. This can decrease erosion in the area. The time and effort you put in now will pay off with a cleaner, greener world. And there's another hidden bonus. It's really fun!

How Does YOUR Garden Grow?

Balcony or Patio Gardening

Train Boston ivy or fruit-bearing vines to run up a trellis on a balcony. Fill a window box with flowers. Place trees, herbs, or flowers in pots on a patio.

Community Gardening

If you live in a high-rise or other type of home without a yard, find out if there's a community garden in your area. Community gardens bring people together to care for a piece of land. Kids are always welcome.

School Garden

If you don't have a place to garden at home, find out if you can make a place at your school. Even if there's not much room available, you can be creative with containers (see above).

Flower Beds

Got grass but no flowers? Ask your parents if you can dig out a flowerbed along the edge of the lawn. Flowers will add color and interest to the yard, while also attracting butterflies and bugs.

Trees

Plant trees! Trees suck carbon out of the atmosphere, leaving the air cleaner. If you live in an urban area, they're great for reducing "heat islands"—places where the pavement and asphalt make the temperature rise.

Bushes

Planting a bush is like building a home for a bunny, bird, or other small creature. They love the shelter that bushes provide. Berry bushes are always popular with the animals—they're like animal snack bars.

Herbs

Spice up your life with some herbs. You can grow them in pots on a sunny windowsill or plant them in the ground. Cook with them for the freshest taste you can get.

Vegetables

Create a produce section in your backyard. You'll be eating healthy all summer and into the winter, too (see page 104).

Imagine hundreds, even thousands of people all gathered together, sharing their ideas and inventions for living in a way that's better for the planet. You don't have to imagine—just go to a green expo! Expo is short for exposition—basically a show. A green expo shows you how to make your house, your car, or your whole life greener. Demonstrations, workshops, and lots of kids' activities are part of most green expos. There are model homes with green roofs, vehicles that run on alternative power, and even green fashion shows! Get your parents to take you and get inspired about what you can do.

TO A GREEN EXPO

NORTH

GOING GREEN EXPOS
Maine, Vermont, and New Hampshire
Learn about solar power, green
energy, and much more.
www.goinggreenexpos.com

GREEN EXPO
Peterborogh, ON
www.greenexpo.ca/index.html

EPIC: THE SUN SUSTAINABLE LIVING EXPO
Vancouver, BC
www.epicexpo.com

GREEN FESTIVAL
Washington, DC
Learn about ways to live with a
lighter footprint.
http://greenfestivals.org

GO GREEN EXPO
New York, NY
Green exhibits, movies, and
marketplace.
www.gogreenexpo.com

MIDWEST

LIVING GREEN EXPO
St. Paul, MN
Workshops, displays, and many
different ideas for living green
(and kids' events and activities).
www.livinggreen.org/index.cfm

GOING GREEN WISCONSIN
Madison, WI
Demonstrations, exhibitons, and fun.
www.channel3000.com/goinggreen

GREEN FESTIVAL
Chicago, IL
Learn to live with a lighter footprint.
http://greenfestivals.org

WEST

SOLAR FIESTA
Albuquerque, NM
Solar workshops and exhibitions.
www.nmsea.org/

RENEWABLE ENERGY ROUNDUP AND GREEN LIVING FAIR
Fredericksburg, TX
Green energy, building, transportation, and fun family events.
http://theroundup.org/index.php

ROCKY MOUNTAIN SUSTAINABILITY FAIR
Fort Collins, CO
Demonstrations, speakers, workshops, and "Planet Youth."
http://sustainablelivingassociation.
org/thefair/

SAN FRANCISCO GREEN FESTIVAL
San Francisco, CA
Learn to live lighter.
http://greenfestivals.org

BETTER LIVING SHOW
Portland, OR
Exhibits on how to make everything
in your life greener.
www.betterlivingshow.org

SOUTH

SOUTHERN ENERGY AND ENVIRONMENT EXPO
Asheville, NC
Everything you want to know about
getting clean, renewable energy into
your life!
www.seeexpo.com

29 Be Ozone Aware

When it comes to ozone (an atmospheric gas), there's the good, the bad, and the ugly. Good ozone is that kind that exists in the upper layer of Earth's atmosphere, helping to block out some of the sun's most harmful rays. Then there's the bad kind—ground level ozone, which is closer to Earth. It's caused by emissions from cars and factories, chemicals, and some natural sources. Bad ozone causes air pollution—the smog that you can see in the air on certain days, especially in the summer. Here's what's ugly about bad ozone—it can really hurt people with asthma and other breathing difficulties or even cause respiratory problems. It also damages trees and crops, and just looks ugly, and smells bad, too. Conserving energy and using the car less are two things you and your family can do to help decrease bad ozone.

Create an Ozone Garden

How is bad ozone affecting your environment? Do an experiment and find out.

First, you'll need to plant at least one bioindicator plant— a plant that's sensitive to the conditions of the atmosphere and reacts when air quality is poor. Try one of the plants on the following page, if they're native to your area.

BIOINDICATOR PLANTS

Mugwort
Big-leaf aster
Red maple
Goldenrod
Tulip tree
Common milkweed
Cut leaf coneflower
Flowering dogwood
Viginia creeper
Evening primrose
Yellow poplar

You need a plant that's young and in good condition. You can use a clay pot if you don't have a garden. Use dirt instead of potting soil. Make sure no pesticides are used anywhere near the plants.

Measure the height of your plant and count the leaves. Make notes about the color of the leaves. Use a magnifying glass to get a close-up look.

Continue to check your plant every week or two weeks to see if it's had any ozone damage. Ozone damage is displayed in several ways: yellowing of the leaves, purple spots under the leaves, or dead leaves. Keep notes about what happens to your plant.

At the same time you're checking your plants, check your area's air-quality index (sometimes available in your local paper or online). You might see a connection between the air quality and the effect on your plant.

30 Choose Nature

Can a game of stickball really save the planet? Can a camping trip change the world? Well, in a way, yes. Imagine a world where everyone was inside, plugged in to electrical outlets all day, fingers mashing away at buttons on video games. It wouldn't really matter if the air and water were clean, if animals had a place to call home, if the planet's temperature was rising—after all, inside is climate controlled. But would anyone really want to live in a world like that? Choosing to surf, backpack, or play soccer rather than play video or computer games may not seem like a big deal. But it makes you an investor in the planet's future. You want the ocean, the woods, and your soccer field to still be there, right? Caring is the first step toward doing something for the environment. And as long as there are kids like you who still care, the planet has somebody fighting for it.

31 Charge It!

If you use a digital camera or play with handheld games, there's a good chance you go through a lot of disposable batteries. But have you ever considered where they go after you dispose of them? If you throw them out with your trash, they'll end up in a landfill, where they'll leak toxins and contaminate the ground. That takes all the fun out using them, doesn't it? Try rechargeable batteries. Yes, they're more expensive than a pack of disposables, but you can recharge them and use them again, saving you money in the end. Yes, you'll have to go a little out of your way to buy rechargables and a charger, but you'll be able to use them for years, so they're worth the extra effort. Need more convincing? Some say rechargeable batteries give you more power than the throw-away kind. Could they also improve your game scores? Try them and find out.

51

32 JOIN FORCES

FIND OUT MORE AT ROOTS AND SHOOTS AT WWW.ROOTSAND-SHOOTS.ORG.

Saving the planet is a big job—call for back up! There are lots of kids like you who care about the environment, and some of them probably go to your school. Talk to your teacher about starting an eco-club. Use the tips on the opposite page to help you get started. If there's not one in your town already, consider starting a chapter of a nationwide or even international group such as Roots and Shoots, which is an organization just for kids that was founded by Jane Goodall, the famous gorilla researcher. You're not alone: we're in this together, and together we are strong.

ECO-CLUB 101

STEP 1: RECRUIT! Get a staff/teacher sponsor for your club. To find members for your club, advertise in the school newsletter, or put posters (made from recycled paper!) up in the common areas, such as the cafeteria (get permission first if you need to). Pick a good time for an informational meeting. During lunch or right before or after school might be good possibilities. If you don't have a big turn out the first time, don't worry—there are lots of factors that could affect turnout. Try another meeting at a different time, or give potential members personal reminders.

STEP 2: ORGANIZE. As a group, decide what your focus will be. Ask the members which issues they care about the most. Decide how the group will work. How often will you meet? Who will be in charge of different activities? Vote or get volunteers for different roles in the group. Give yourself a name!

STEP 3: PRIORITIZE. Now that you know which issues you care about, decide which are most important to work on first.

STEP 4: TAKE ACTION. "Think Globally, Act Locally" is a well known saying and a good way to start focusing your effort. Partner with other local environmental groups, or other clubs in your school to organize projects and events.

EVENT AND ACTIVITY IDEAS

- Tree planting
- Recycling program
- Trail clearing
- River clean up
- Park clean up
- School energy audit
- School composting
- Letter writing campaign
- School garden
- Schoolyard habitat
- "Teach in" about environmental issues
- Adopt a road, watershed, wetland, etc., and help care for it
- Petition the school system to buy paper with high recycled content
- Farms to Schools program

BE A PICKER UPPER

You see a piece of trash on the ground and think, "That's really bad. Who would throw a piece of trash on the ground?" Then you keep walking. You may not have even realized it, but somewhere in your head, you could have been thinking, "I didn't put it there. I don't have to pick it up." And you're right. You don't *have* to. But you may actually want to. When you care about the Earth, you change your actions to help protect the planet. But you can't just stop there. Sometimes you're going to have to care about actions that other people take, too. Instead of "It's not my trash," think, "It *is* my Earth, and I want it to be clean." Cleaning up trash can help make your neighborhood a better place and protect the wildlife that lives in your neighborhood, too. People will notice, and might think twice before they litter again. Hey, people might even feel guilty walking past trash if they notice you and your friends picking it up. If you feel lonely in your clean-up efforts, create a clean-up team and get your friends in on the fun.

33

CALCULATE YOUR CARBON

To calculate your carbon, try one of these sites:

www.carbonfootprint.com
www.nature.org
www.climatecrisis.net/
takeaction/carboncalculator

You know your shoe size, but do you know the size of your carbon footprint? A carbon footprint measures how much greenhouse gas is released into the environment based on how you live. Simple, everyday actions, such as being driven to school or washing your clothes will have an impact on the environment. The trick is to try to make that impact as minimal as possible. In other words, make a lighter footprint. You can find out what your family's footprint looks like by going to one of the many online carbon calculators and filling in the details about your life— if your family has a car, what kind is it? How big is your home and what kind of energy do you use for it? When you go on vacation, how do you travel and where do you go? You'll get a better idea of how your actions can contribute to global warming and find ideas on how you can tread more lightly.

SEND PACKAGING PACKING

You've seen this before: a tiny, tiny little toy in a big, big, box surrounded by layers of cardboard, plastic, twisty-ties, and other filler material. So what do you do with all that stuff when you've finally gotten the toy out? Right into the garbage. Packaging accounts for more than half the paper produced in the U.S. and almost half of it ends up un-recycled, in landfills. That means that half the trees that are cut down aren't cut to make products that are used. They're cut just to make something that's MEANT TO BE THROWN AWAY. And boy, do we. Each person throws away around 300 pounds (136 kg) of packaging every year. You can do something about this. First, look for products with less packaging or at least packaging that can be recycled. You can also write to the companies that make your favorite things, and tell them you're not going to buy their products unless they cut down on the packaging (see page 112). And if they don't change? See if you can live without those favorite things. It might be easier than you think. Don't forget, you're paying for the packaging and the product. Why pay for what you throw away?

For more information, go to
www.dogwoodalliance.org.

36 START A SWAP MEET

How can you turn a household chore into a party where you help the Earth and get free stuff? It's easy: start a swap meet. Empty out your closet, drawers, and shelves. Make a pile of things you don't want anymore or don't play with anymore. Be realistic: if you haven't worn/played with/picked it up in over a year, you probably never will. Once you have some "stock," invite your friends to come over with their unwanted stuff. Provide some snacks and a big space for swapping. Swaps work better if you have rules, so let everyone have a chance to look at what's available before grabbing stuff. Appoint an adult "referee" who'll help mediate decisions if more than one person wants the same thing. Think creatively. You may not wear a certain sweater, but you could felt the sweater or turn it into a pillow. If you have stuff left over at the end of the swap, drop it off with a local charity. No money is exchanged, everyone gets something new, and nothing is wasted. It's all good.

Long before there were chemical cleaners made in factories, people cleaned their homes the natural way. While strong chemical cleaners do the job, they usually have side effects. They can cause allergies, trigger asthma attacks, and release toxins into the air, ground, or water. Unlock the power of lemon! Make the world better through baking soda! Using natural ingredients to clean is also way more fun that using store-bought cleaners—you can turn your kitchen into a lab, experimenting with different amounts of each substance to test the results. Clean, natural, and fun all together.

37 Clean Green

Check out soapnuts, which come from the Chinese soapberry tree and contain a natural detergent. Put them in a sack in your washing machine, and then compost them when they're all used up. You can find out more about soapnuts by doing an online search with the terms "soapnuts," or "soapberry tree."

Clean & Green

INSTEAD OF	USE
All-purpose cleaner	Baking soda mixed with warm water in a spray bottle
Dishwashing liquid	Lemon juice diluted with water
Window cleaner	White vinegar diluted with water
Carpet stain remover	Cornstarch mixed with water into a paste
Toilet bowl cleaner	Pure white vinegar

Lemon
Removes soap scum from sinks and tubs; cleans glasses and dishes.

White Vinegar
Mixed with water, it can clean counter-tops and stove tops. Undiluted, it can be used to clean toilets and shower walls. Mixed with a little rubbing alcohol, it can clean mirrors and windows. If you've opened a bottle of vinegar you know…the smell is strong. You may be concerned that the smell is just as bad as the dirt it's cleaning! Don't worry. The smell disappears once the vinegar is dry.

Baking Soda
Baking soda can be scrubbed onto sinks to remove build-up. It's also a natural drain-clog remover.

Have you ever noticed that after you've played a million different video games, they all start to seem the same after a while? You must escape the (choose an adjective: wicked, evil, mutant) (choose a noun: wizard, troll, robot) in order to protect the (choose a noun: magical tokens, princess, computer chip) and make your way to the (choose a noun: hidden treasure, secret island, new world). Why not try a game with a twist: helping your actual planet, for real? There are some new games out there that help you learn to solve real planet problems, and they're fun, too! Instead of trading imaginary monster cards, why not trade endangered species? Or help Chibi Robo, a little robot clean up a polluted park? Be the first one of your friends to give an eco-game a try.

CHECK OUT

- ★ www.planetgreengame.com for a reality-based eco-challenge game
- ★ http://simcitysocieties.ea.com for a chance to build the ideal world
- ★ http://xeko.com to learn how to collect cards and play Xeko, an endangered animal trading card game
- ★ Adventure Ecology is a free online game at http://mission control.adventureecology.com

39
PLUG THE LEAKS

CONSIDER INSULATING YOUR WINDOWS WITH PLASTIC SHEETING DURING WINTER.

A cool breeze coming through your window can feel really refreshing—but not if it's winter! Air leaking out through windows and under doors can make homes up to 30 % less energy efficient. You can keep the heat in and cool air out (and vice versa in the summer) by tracking down and plugging up those leaks. Run your finger along the edge of each window and door in your house. Can you feel a breeze? If so, your house could be more efficient. If there are visible holes, get a parent to help you fill them with caulking, and use weather stripping around doors and windows. Look for other places where air can go in and out, such as attic hatches, pet doors, window-mounted air conditioners, and fireplace dampers. Once you've sealed it all up, your home will be more energy efficient and more comfortable, too.

40 Veg Out

You don't have to be a vegetarian to be a planet protector, but it helps. Raising animals to eat creates a lot of waste and uses a lot of energy. Studies show that the fuel used to make a single hamburger is equal to driving 20 miles (32 km) in a car. And the amount of water used to produce a pound of beef is roughly equal to all the water you use showering in an entire year. Vegetarian food is healthy, tasty, and is easier on the planet—and those are just a few of its benefits. If you're not ready to go "cold turkey" on meat, try cutting meat out of a few meals at a time. Suggest a family Vegetarian Night once a week. Make it a time to try new and creative recipes. Or try one of the many vegetarian meat substitute products.

41 Stay Dirty!

What are you planning to do with the shirt you're wearing? Wear it once, and then throw it in the hamper (or on the floor for someone else to pick up)? Unless you rolled around in the dirt, spilled a cup of lemonade on yourself, or wiped your nose on the sleeve, there's a good chance that shirt is still clean enough to wear again. Every time you run the washing machine, around 41 gallons (156 L) of water go down the drain. If it's warm or hot water, your home uses energy to heat the water as well. If it's just a tiny spot of dirt, use a wash rag and a tiny bit of soap to clean it off. Sending your clothes through the washing machine less often will make them last longer, too, cutting down on your need to spend more money to replace them and the resources used to create them. So, unless your jeans smell like dog, hang them up and wear them again later in the week. You'll have less work to do if it's your week to help with laundry.

42 Switch It

A couple of little switches can make a big difference in the amount of energy you use in your home. Switch the lights off when you leave the room. Make sure they're all switched off in your house when you go to bed at night. That goes for the TV, stereo, and ceiling fans, too. Switch from regular old *incandescent* light bulbs to *compact fluorescent* light bulbs (CFLs). If everyone in the U.S. switched just one old bulb to compact fluorescent, it would be like taking 800,000 cars off the road, and enough energy would be saved to power 3 million homes for a year! Don't just switch the bulb—get a parent to switch the fixtures to Energy Star fixtures—they help cut greenhouse gas emissions even further. Isn't it amazing what a little switch can do?

Handle CFLs very carefully. They contain harmful gases, and if one breaks, you'll need an adult to clean it up. When a CFL finally stops working, contact your local landfill for instructions for proper disposal.

43 BE ONE IN A MILLION

There's a new idea sprouting up all over the place: let's see if we can plant a million trees! Kids and adults all over North America are planting trees and keeping a tally so that it's clear when the million mark is reached. When you plant a tree with your family, a school group, or just by yourself, let your effort be known—be one in a million. Just go to one of the web sites below, learn about the best trees to plant, where to get them, or how to start them from seed. Then register your tree. You could make tree-planting into a great school challenge— which club, class, or grade can plant the most?

4-H Club Million Trees Project
www.4hmilliontrees.org/

Million Trees L.A. (Los Angeles)
www.milliontreesla.org

Million Trees New York
www.milliontreesnyc.org

Million Trees Salt Lake County (UT)
www.milliontrees.slco.org

44 GET SOME NEW PETS

Worms might just be the perfect pets. They don't wake you up in the morning to take them for a walk. They don't chew up your favorite shoes. And most important, they help you get rid of the garbage. Sure, they're not the cuddliest of creatures, and you can't play Frisbee with them, but they're about as eco-friendly as a pet can get. Buy some worms and make a little home for them (see page 67). Collect food scraps from your kitchen (old lettuce leaves, apple cores,

coffee grinds, leftovers, for example) and feed the worms. In time, they'll eat their body weight in food each day and make castings (fancy word for "poop") that you can spread around in your garden to make your plants grow like crazy. Voilá—you're *vermicomposting*! If your vermicomposting experiment goes well at home, why not start one at school?

FOODS WORMS DON'T LIKE

Watermelon rinds
Banana peels
Meat scraps
Bone
Spicy foods like onion or garlic

SETTING UP YOUR WORM BIN

The worm bin is the final resting place for your old kitchen scraps and home sweet home for your pet worms. If you don't have much space, your bin can be as small as a bucket. You can make your own bin out of wood, or use an old plastic or metal container. To make castings, worms need only a few things: food, moisture, and oxygen. So if you use a pre-made container, it's important to make sure it has a system for letting in oxygen and letting out excess moisture. If the bin is too wet, it will start to smell.

Line your bin with moist shredded newspaper or computer paper scraps to make a "bed." Add in some crushed eggshells, clean play sand (the kind used in sandboxes), or wet shredded cardboard. A small amount of soil is okay, too. Put in the worms and then your food scraps. If your bin has a lid, put it in place, or you can use a plastic garbage bag over the top. Feed your worms every week or so and add new bedding as it breaks down, checking to make sure it stays moist. In three to six months, it's time to collect the castings. Dump your bin onto a plastic sheet and put new bedding in it. Put your worms back in the bin and spread the castings around the base of your plants.

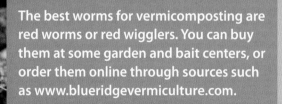

The best worms for vermicomposting are red worms or red wigglers. You can buy them at some garden and bait centers, or order them online through sources such as www.blueridgevermiculture.com.

45 Green Your School Supplies

Are you looking for a way to make an impression at school? Be the first kid in your class to write with a pen made from corn. Be the only kid with a pencil made from an old pair of jeans, or crayons made from soy wax. And you'll really catch people's eyes—and noses—with a *bubble-gum scented* pencil made from recycled newspaper! A binder made from corrugated cardboard is eco-friendly and fun to decorate. And while notebooks and paper with high recycled content might not guarantee good grades, they're guaranteed to be more Earth-friendly than the ordinary kind. What's not cool to take to school? Pens, binders, or backpacks made with vinyl—creating vinyl releases harmful toxins into the air, making a very bad impression on the planet.

Check with your local office supply store to find out which recycled and eco-friendly school supply options they offer. You can also find supplies online by typing in "recycled school supplies." (But try to locate a local vendor.)

Ah, the landfill. It may not be top on your list of destinations, but if there's any place that can really give you a picture about why we need to stop consuming so much, this is it. You might have heard the facts before. Each individual in the U.S. and Canada produces an average of 4.6 pounds (2 kg) of garbage per day, contributing to a total of more than 251 tons (226 t) of annual garbage, 34% of which is paper (that means it's not being recycled). But until you see the acres and acres of garbage piled high, those figures might not really hit home. When you tell your friends about your landfill visit, here are some things you *won't* be saying: "What we really need in this world is more *stuff*!" "Why bother recycling?" "Who cares what happens to my trash after it leaves my house?" What you will be saying is, "Let me tell you a few things about garbage…"

46

SEE FOR YOURSELF

47 Host Some Bats

Bats are nature's own pest control system. They gobble up mosquitoes, gnats, and beetles like candy. In fact, an average bat is said to be able to eat up to 300 insects a night! With bats around, you won't need bug sprays or insecticides that can leave traces of chemicals in your garden and kill natural predators. But how can you get bats to stick around? Build or purchase a bat house where they can roost. Hosting bats in your yard helps preserve the natural order of things, and lets you enjoy the outdoors without all those pesky mosquito bites.

Insects are a bat's favorite food. So, if you have sweet-smelling flowers in your garden (honeysuckle, lemon balm, or mint, for example), a pond or other water feature that attracts insects, you'll have an easier time attracting bats. A compost pile is good for your garden and also good for bats—they love to eat the bugs that eat the compost.

For free bat house plans, go to www.batcon.org or www.nwf.org.

Bat House Basics

Use untreated wood for your bat house (bats are sensitive to chemicals). The wood should be a little rough, too, so that it will be easier for the bats to grip onto it. You can also try adding window screening, which serves the same purpose.

The outside dimensions of your bat house should be at least 2 feet (60 cm) tall by 14 inches (36 cm) wide, with a 3- to 6-inch (7.6 x 15 cm) "landing pad." Inside the box, you'll need to create partitions—little slots where bats can snuggle in. Each partition should be between 3/4 and 1 inch (2 and 2.5 cm) wide. There should be a narrow slit on the bottom for bats to use as a door.

You bat house should be mounted in a place that gets at least 4 hours of sunlight a day.

Northern bats like houses that are painted dark. Mexican free-tailed bats—found in the South—need shade and cool temperatures in summer, especially in desert areas.

The higher up you put your bat house, the better. Experts suggest a using 15 to 24-foot (4.5 to 7 m) pole, or hanging your bat house 12 to 15 feet (3.5 x 4.5 m) up a tree or on the side of a building.

How do you know if bats have moved into your bat house? You might hear "chittering" sounds coming from inside the box during the day, or see bat droppings on the ground near the box. You can even look in it very briefly with a flashlight without disturbing them—just be quiet and don't touch the house.

48 GET CRAFTY!

To some, it may look like an old shoebox. To you, it's a home for your shell collection. While others see an empty mint tin, you see a clever desk-organizing device. Empty containers are not trash—they're craft projects waiting to happen. Reusing stuff you'd otherwise throw away takes recycling to a whole new level. Before you toss it, look at it differently. Could it serve another purpose? Think creatively. You'll save money, have fun, and help the planet.

WHAT CAN YOU DO WITH....

BABY FOOD JARS

Paint storage: store paint you've already mixed
Decorated votive candleholder: use glass paint to decorate the sides and stick a candle inside
Snow globe: glue an item to the inside bottom, fill it with water and glitter and put the lid back on

TISSUE BOXES

Picture frame: decorate the sides and put a picture in the opening on top
CD holder: cut the top off, decorate the sides, and store CDs in it
Guitar: put rubber bands around it and play

MINT TINS

Picture frame: decorate the outside and glue a picture to the inside bottom of the tin

Gift box: decorate the outside and put a small present inside

Change purse: paint it and carry change inside it

Jewelry case: store your earrings in them

Storage box: store beads and other small craft materials inside them

OLD JEANS

Purse: cut off the legs and sew the openings; hang a strap from the top

Shorts: cut the legs at the length you want your shorts to be

OLD CDS

Mosaic: break up the CD and use it in a mosaic project

Mobile: hang CDs from string on a hanger

OLD HARDCOVER BOOKS

Secret stash: cut a hole in the middle and put stuff inside it

Book purse: use the covers as the sides of a purse

MISMATCHED SOCKS

Sock monkey: cut different parts of two socks, stuff them, and sew them together

Sock puppet: put a face where your foot used to be

SHOEBOX

Shadow box: set it on its side and create a display

Jewelry box: decorate the outside and store your jewelry in it

Temporary turtle home: you can watch your new friend for a bit before letting him go back to his natural home

The sea has always been a source of plenty for humans—plenty of fish, plenty of shells, plenty enough for everyone, right? While our oceans are vast, its resources aren't never-ending. Some species have been so over-fished that they're practically extinct, and some methods of fishing for one kind of fish is hurting other forms of marine life. Treat the seas as respectfully as you treat the land.

If you eat fish, ask whoever shops for your food to look for the Marine Stewardship Council certification to make sure the fish is safe to eat and was harvested in a responsible way.

If you see trash on the beach, pick it up. If it gets carried out to sea, it can hurt sea turtles (see page 75), fish, seabirds, and other wildlife.

If you go snorkeling or scuba diving, look, but don't touch the coral reefs—they're a fragile ecosystem that can easily be destroyed.

Don't walk on dunes—that leads to beach erosion.

If you have fish in an aquarium at home, buy only those that have a Marine Aquarium Council certification.

What's so special about sea turtles? Well, for one thing, they've been on the planet for 150 million years. That means sea turtles beat the odds and endured changes to the Earth that wiped out much bigger, tougher animals such as dinosaurs. Several ice ages didn't kill them, and neither did their many predators in the sea and on land. But after surviving all these big threats, sea turtles might be done in by human garbage. A simple piece of fishing line thrown or lost in the ocean may seem harmless, but a sea turtle can easily become entangled in it and die. To a sea turtle, a floating plastic bag looks like one of its favorite foods: jellyfish. But when the turtle tries to eat it, it'll choke. What can you do to help? As you're walking along the beach, don't just pick up shells, pick up trash. Every time you do, you eliminate a threat to a sea turtle, and give this amazing species a chance at surviving for another 150 million years.

For more information on sea turtles and what you can do to help them, go to www.cccturtle.org.

50

Save the Sea Turtles

51 PLAY FAIR

TO FIND OUT MORE ABOUT FAIR TRADE, GO TO: WWW.OXFAM.ORG.UK/COOLPLANET/KIDSWEB/FAIRTRADE/INDEX.HTM

Fair trade: It means that the people in other countries who harvest the bananas you eat, the cocoa for your chocolate, or those who make your soccer ball got a fair price for their work. When trade is fair, poor people can live a better life and get ahead. That's great for them, but how does that help the environment? Fair-trade farmers respect their local environments and protect local habitats. Because they can make money through farming or crafting, they don't have to move to cities to work in big polluting factories or cut down trees in their own communities just to get by. When trade is fair, the Earth and its inhabitants live more harmoniously, keeping everything in a better balance. Look for the fair-trade label at stores.

A TALE OF TWO BANANAS

Same fruit, different system.
Which banana would you rather eat?

FREE-TRADE BANANA

◆ Grown on a plantation that was created by chopping down natural habitat, displacing animal habitat, and causing soil erosion that contaminates rivers.

◆ Grown with pesticides.

◆ Production creates tons of waste that isn't properly disposed of and contaminates local rivers.

◆ Workers who harvest it are paid only pennies for their work.

FAIR-TRADE BANANA

◆ Farmers protect ecosystems and avoid cutting down trees and causing erosion.

◆ Farmers reduce the use of chemical pesticides or grow bananas organically.

◆ Wastes are composted.

◆ Farmers receive a better wage for their harvest.

52
ASK THE BIG QUESTIONS

It's always good to ask questions, even if you're only asking yourself. Before you buy something, trying asking yourself: Do I *want* this or Do I *need* this? A lot of the issues facing our planet right now could be solved if everyone just stuck to what they needed instead of what they wanted; if everyone took just enough, but not more than their share. Try making a list of your wants versus your needs. Look at each item carefully. Think about how you can achieve your needs without bringing more stuff into the world. For example, you probably need a piece of equipment for your sports activity or an instrument to practice on, but could you get a used one instead of buying a new one? You need to stay warm in the winter, but do you have to buy a new coat? Could you use the one from last year? Asking the big questions will not only make you a smarter consumer, it will make your impact on the planet lighter—something we all really *need* to do.

53 Green Your Grandparents

With age comes wisdom, and there's a good chance that your grandparents know a lot more about certain things than you will ever know. But that doesn't mean your grandparents don't have a thing or two to learn from *you*. Now that you're an enviro-expert (see page 26), you have plenty of wisdom about energy efficiency, recycling, global warming, and so many other things. On your next visit to gram and gramps, do a quick check of their light bulbs—do they know they could save money and help the environment if they use CFLs (see page 64)? Are there any leaky faucets you could offer to fix? You'll get extra points for helpfulness, too. And if anyone can convince them to trade in that gas-guzzling sedan for a hybrid, it's you. (I mean really, when's the last time your grandparents said "no" to you!?)

For more information on native plants, go to http://plants.usda.gov and search for "native plants." Or go to www.nanps.org.

No matter how long you've lived in your neighborhood, there are probably some residents who've been there longer—the plants. When the first settlers arrived in North America, there were no short-cut yards of grass or orderly flower beds. Just native plant species growing wild. Native plants are still best for the environment. They require less water than *invasive* or exotic (non-native) species, provide homes for animals, don't need pesticides, and can live with less fertilizer. They're a natural choice for your family's garden. Learn which plants are native to your area by checking online, going to the library, or asking an older neighbor who has lived in the area most of his life. Then, look for a nursery that carries native plants. Native plants will also help you attract something very interesting to your garden—native critters.

55 Bring Your Own

You're with your mom or dad at the grocery check-out when the familiar question pops up: Paper or plastic? It's not as easy an answer as you may think. Paper bag manufacturers may tell you that their bags are biodegradable. They won't tell you, however, that it takes a lot of greenhouse gases to make them. Plastic bag makers will tell you that their bags don't require a lot of energy to produce. They may forget to mention that the bags will be around for hundreds of years. Your greenest answer: Neither, we brought our own bags.

Take along your own cloth or recycled material bags to the store. They help make your footprint a little lighter and they also make great gifts (see below).

SOME BAG FACTS

✔ 1 tree = 700 grocery bags.
Think how many bags leave your grocery store in a single hour. That's just one store in one place.... Multiply that by all the grocery stores in the country and you're talking about a lot of trees.

✔ Both paper and plastic bags can be recycled, but only 10% to 15% of paper bags and 1% to 3% of plastic bags are being recycled.

Ask your grocery store if they have a plastic bag recycling bin. If not, leave a comment in their suggestions box. (Most grocery stores have them.)

✔ It takes more than four times as much energy to manufacture a paper bag as it does to manufacture a plastic bag.

That sounds pretty good. However, plastic bags create four times as much solid waste.

✔ To make all the bags we use each year, it takes 14 million trees for paper and 12 million barrels of oil for plastic.

All this for something you don't need as soon as you walk into your kitchen. If you have lots of leftover shopping bags, don't throw them in the garbage. Recycle them by turning them into garbage bags.

✔ Since plastic is cheaper to produce, most stores use them. The average family uses nearly 1,500 plastic bags per year.

Talk with your family and tell them it's not okay to be "average!"

56 Show Companies You MEAN BUSINESS

Have you ever heard about the power of the pocketbook? It means that whatever you spend your money on gains power, importance, and a little thing politicians call "clout." So why not use your pocketbook power to support products that are trying to do right by the planet. You can decide to use your allowance to buy a treat from the bulk aisle of the grocery store, eliminating extra packaging. Or, choose products that donate profits to causes you care about, that support family farms, that offer fair wages to the people who create them. And what can you do about companies that aren't making real efforts to take the environment into consideration? Don't give them your money, and convince your friends and their friends and so on not to give them their money. Before you know it, you have a boycott on your hands. And you thought a major company wouldn't listen to a kid like you. As the old saying goes "the buck stops" with you. You're in charge of your choices, and your choices make a difference.

57 Get Competitive

As if helping the planet wasn't reward enough, you can actually win prizes for it. As governments, companies, and nonprofits look for new ways to solve the Earth's problems, they've realized that kids have great ideas, and they want to recognize and honor kids' contributions. By yourself or with a team, come up with a project and submit your results to an environmental challenge or contest. Even if you don't get an award, you'll know that you're a winner because you've done something good for the planet.

THE LEXUS ENVIRONMENTAL CHALLENGE

Open to teams of middle-school or high-school students, the challenge awards scholarship money to the team with the most innovative environmental projects.
www.scholastic.com/lexus/

PRESIDENT'S ENVIRONMENTAL YOUTH AWARDS

Open to individuals or groups in the U.S.
www.epa.gov/enviroed/peya/

THE SUNLIGHT ECO-ACTION KIDS AWARD

Canadian kids ages 6 to 10 are eligible.
www.sunlightecoactionkids.ca

ACTION FOR NATURE INTERNATIONAL YOUNG ECO-HERO AWARD

Available to kids ages 8 to 16 for creative projects that help the environment.
www.actionfornature.org/eco-hero/

GO GREEN INITIATIVE GREEN SCHOOLS AWARD

How green can you get your school? See if you can become a "School of the Week." www.gogreen.org

58 FLIP IT!

A single piece of paper…so many possibilities—and that's just on the front! When you flip the paper over, you can let your imagination start all over again on the other side. Using both sides of a piece of paper just makes sense—two sides are better than one. But don't stop there. If you're printing something from your computer, you might be able to save even more paper. Some software programs can print two or more pages on the front of one sheet of paper. Use the "help" function of your word-processing program to look for this option. Then you can print and flip the paper and do the same on the other side.

On average, Americans use the most paper each year: 650 pounds (300 kg) of paper each year, which uses up more than 4 billion trees a year.

59 PURGE THE PETROL

Do you know which products in your house are petroleum-based? How about those candles in your living room, the lotion in your bathroom, the detergent in your laundry room, and even the chocolate candy in your kitchen! Surprised? There are probably more things in your home made with petroleum-derived ingredients than aren't. But petroleum is NOT a renewable resource and petroleum-based products aren't biodegradable. Look for plant-based products (see the list below). Plants ARE a renewable resource—they're safer for the environment and they biodegrade. More plants, less drilling—it's a step in the right direction.

CHOOSE	INSTEAD OF
Soy or beeswax candles	Paraffin candles
Plant-based lotion and soap	Petroleum-based cosmetics
Organic chocolate	Chocolate containing paraffin
Natural cleaners	Petroleum-based detergents
Organic fabric	Synthetic fabric
Glass or metal	Plastic
Soy ink cartridges	Conventional ink cartridges

GO Watch Your Water

If more than two-thirds of the planet's surface is covered in water, why does it matter how much of it we use? Because of all that water, less than 1% is usable for human purposes, such as drinking, bathing, and cooking. That 1% is used by humans, animals, businesses, and farms. In many places worldwide, there's not enough water to go around. And in most industrialized countries (like yours) each person uses an average of 100 gallons (380 L) of water each day! Work with your family on keeping an eye on the water you use each day. This will help keep it flowing to the places that need it most.

WAYS TO WATCH YOUR WATER

- Take a quick shower instead of a bath.
- Even better, take a speed shower! See if you can be in and out in under 5 minutes.
- Turn off the faucet while you're brushing your teeth or washing the dishes. You don't need running water for either—just a splash at the beginning and/or end.
- Lose the leaks. If you have drips or leaks from your faucet or toilet, get them fixed. They not only waste water, they cost your family money.

- Only run your dishwasher when it's completely full. That goes for the washing machine, too.
- With most newer dishwashers, you don't have to rinse the dishes before putting them in. Try it out with yours. Think about it: less work and less water used!

- Buy or make a rain barrel (see page 106) and use it to water your plants.
- Using a hose or sprinkler system uses up to 6 gallons (23 L) of water a minute! If you need a sprinkler, find a "smart" one that's programmed to shut off when the grass has had enough.
- Give your dog a bath on the grass— that way the water won't go to waste.

- Two glasses of water are used to clean each glass of water brought to your table at a restaurant. Let your server know that you only want water if you order it.
- Ask your parents to switch to Energy Star appliances in your home. They use much less water than their alternatives.
- If the toilets in your home are more than 20 years old, convince your parents to switch to low-flow toilets. Or, fill a plastic 2 liter or half-gallon drink container (remove all paper labels) halfway with sand, gravel, or pebbles, and then add some water for more weight. Seal the container and place it in the tank away from all the moving parts. You could save at least 1 gallon (3.8 L) per flush!
- Grow drought-tolerant plants in your garden (see page 107).

61 MAP YOUR ECOSYSTEM

An ecosystem can be as big as a desert or as small as what you find under a single rock. Wherever living things exist together and interact with the elements (weather, rocks and minerals, the air, water), you'll find an ecosystem. Your home and your backyard (if you have one) can be part of an ecosystem or contain ecosystems. Looking at ecosystems helps us understand how all living things depend on each other, and how our actions can affect so many different forms of life. Once you have a handle on your ecosystem, you can make more observations about how human activity might affect it.

For more ideas on experiments you can do, go to
http://nationalzoo.si.edu/Education/ConservationCentral/walk/default.cfm

START SMALL. Look at your immediate surroundings, such as your home and its environment or your school and its grounds. What living things do you find? Take an inventory of the plants, animals, and other features that you see. Use guidebooks to help you identify them. What kind of tree is that? What kind of bird? What kind of bugs? Are there different types of soil? What does the soil look like? Sandy? Moist? Dark?

INVESTIGATE FURTHER. Pick up rocks and look underneath—has anything decided to make a home there? Check the surface of the rock—perhaps some moss has started to live on top of it. Look on tree trunks for signs of other life forms as well. Listen—can you hear animals that you can't see?

EXPAND OUT. As you go from your home, observe the neighborhood or other parts of your area. What kind of trees are there? What patterns of development and open space do you observe?

IMAGINE. What would happen if…someone took away the rock that the bugs had lived under? Where would they go? What would happen to the animals that eat the bugs? If they left, how would that affect the plants? How would it affect you? How would it affect other nearby ecosystems? What would happen if they turned the park down the street into houses?

MAP. Make a map of the ecosystem you observed. Use arrows and words, if you like, to show how all the living things interact with each other.

OBSERVE. Keep tracking your ecosystem to see how human actions affect it. Take notes and make observations. Can what you've seen tie in to what's happening to the planet in general?

62
Practice
Extreme Recycling

Put a little challenge into your recycling by going beyond the ordinary. Using your recycling for building projects is one way to start (see page 72), but don't stop there! How many uses can you come up with for dryer lint? What can you do with an old pair of tennis shoes? Or an old sweater? Think outside the box and be creative. You'll find that you won't be able to look at your old things the same way again. And you'll be spending way less time in stores looking for new things.

Super Recyclers!

SHOES

Use old shoes as planters. Fill them with dirt and put plants inside.

Send them to a shoe-recycling program, such as Reuse-a-Shoe (check http://letmeplay.com/reuseashoe).

GLASSES

Even if you get a new prescription, someone else might be able to use your old pair. Check out an eyeglass-recycling center such as www.lionsclubs.org.

SWEATERS

If the sweater is made from wool, you can shrink it in the washer and dryer and turn it into felt to use it for a project, such as a making a winter hat.

Unravel the yarn and make something else from it. Use a seam ripper or other device to take the sweater apart, and then wrap the yarn around a piece of cardboard as you unravel it.

Cut it into pieces to make a pillow, hat, or purse.

BIKES

Give a bike to an organization such as Earn-A-Bike, which will let a kid learn how to fix up the bike and keep it.
Check www.ibike.org for more info.

DRYER LINT

Use lint as mulch. Set your lint around a newly planted seed. The fibers in the lint will biodegrade and nourish the plant.

Make dryer lint clay. Mix ½ cup of dryer lint with 1 cup of water, ½ cup flour, and a few drops of vegetable oil. Cook it on the stove over low heat until it starts to stick together. Take it off the stove, and mix in food coloring if you want to color it. Set it on top of old newspapers to dry for a few days. Use it like papier-maché or salt dough.

Use lint as stuffing. Not to eat—to use for stuffing pillows, sock animals, or other sewn craft projects. You can even leave it outside and birds will take it to "stuff" their nests.

63 TRACK YOUR STUFF

Your shoes, your sheets, your socks… Where does your stuff come from and how did it get to you? Making stuff and sending it all over the world has a huge effect on the environment. The farther stuff has to travel, the more energy is used, and the more polluted the Earth becomes. See if you can find out where the objects in your home were made. Some of them will have labels, others you might have to guess, and still others are made up of materials that came from many different places around the globe. Once you've checked out where your stuff comes from, watch *The Story of Stuff* (www.storyofstuff.com). It's a short movie that will tell you just about everything you need to know about stuff—where it comes from and where it goes when we're done with it. Most of all, it makes you *think* about stuff.

MADE in the USA

```
1  58001 60012  0
```
MADE IN CHINA

Buy a world map, hang it up, and place a map pin
on the location of all your stuff. How much of what
you own is actually local?

For tips on how to green your classroom, visit the Green Squad at www.nrdc.org/greensquad.

64 Green Your Classroom

Ah, your classroom—your home away from home. Some days, you probably spend *more* time there than you do in your own room. While you don't have as much control there as you do at home, there are simple things you can do to make your classroom greener. Increase the natural light. If there are curtains or shades on the windows, open them up. It will save energy, and studies say that you'll even get better grades (see page 38). Make sure there's a recycling bin in your classroom and volunteer to empty it. If handouts are used, ask the teachers to photocopy on both sides. Do a classroom garbage audit (see page 135). If you want to have more impact, start an eco-club. (See page 52 for tips.) Today your classroom, tomorrow the whole school!

65 PLAY GREEN

True or false: Every form of outdoor recreation is eco-friendly. You might be surprised to learn that the answer is "false." While getting outdoors is a great start, what you choose to do when you get there matters, too. Spending time on the beach or trail is awesome, but do it on your feet or on a bike, not in an ATV (all terrain vehicle)—they can severly harm already fragile eco-systems. A blanket of fresh-fallen snow is the best kind of winter fun—enjoy it on skis or a snowboard instead of a snowmobile, which pollutes the air with emissions and noise. When you want to get out on the water, skip the powerboat or personal watercraft—try a kayak, canoe, or windsurfer instead. Discover a new nature-friendly sport. Climbing, backpacking, sailing, surfing, camping, snowboarding, and biking are just a few of the ways to enjoy the great outdoors without harming the environment. Think low-noise, low-impact, low-emissions, high-fun recreation in the great outdoors.

Biodiversity "hotspots" are places with the most amazing plants and animals in the world. They are also the places most likely feeling the heat these days. The forests of Central America—home to howler monkeys, ocelots, and jaguars—are disappearing, leaving these cool animals endangered (seven species from this hotspot have already become extinct). The tropical Andes, the world's most diverse region, is being damaged by oil exploration, logging, and mining, among other things. Hundreds of species of birds, amphibians, mammals, and plants in this region are threatened. What can you do to help? Spread the word about these hotspots. Do a report or presentation at your school. Host an Endangered Species Day event in your class—invite other classes to attend. Write a letter to the companies that exploit these areas and make *them* feel the heat!

Check out www.biodiversityhotspots.org for more information.

Who can you write? Check www.ran.org/new/kidscorner/ kid_s_action for ideas and more information.

Endangered Species Day is celebrated in May. Check www.stopextinction.org to find out which day it will be held this year.

66
Help a Hotspot

67 Don't Eat Poison Apples

If only Snow White had had this advice—she and the Prince could have started their happily ever after years earlier. While commercial pesticides don't pack quite the punch that Snow's stepmother put into her poison apple, they can have trace amounts of toxins that cause harmful side effects on your garden and possibly on you. Pesticides kill "bad" bugs, such as aphids, that eat your plants, as well as "good" bugs, such as ladybugs, that eat bad bugs. Instead, try making your own garden insecticides with natural ingredients. Insecticidal soaps, as natural insecticides are called, will keep bad bugs away without harming beneficial bugs. Use one of the recipes on the opposite page to give your apples, lettuce, basil, tomatoes, and even flowers a "happily ever after" in your garden.

Keep Bugs at Bay the Natural Way

Simple Soap Spray

Mix 1 teaspoon liquid eucalyptus soap (found at natural food stores) with 1 quart (1 L) of warm water. Pour the mixture into a spray bottle and shake to use.

Note: Don't use just any old liquid soap for this recipe—some soaps contain lye, which could burn the leaves off your plants. Stay with pure eucalyptus if you can find it.

Spicy Insecticidal Soap

Ingredients

1 gallon (3.8 L) of hot water
8 cloves of garlic (pressed and crushed)
1 tablespoon cayenne pepper
1 teaspoon castile soap
Empty milk or water jug
Cheesecloth
Mixing bowl with pour lip
Spray bottle

Mix the spices and soap in the jug. Let the mixture sit for a day or two. Strain it through the cheesecloth over the bowl. Pour the mixture into the spray bottle and spray. This mixture will maintain its effectiveness for a few weeks.

Stop the Fungus Among Us

If you see a fungus (yuck!) starting to grow on a plant, mix a few teaspoons of baking soda in a spray bottle filled with warm water. It should get rid of the fungus in a few days.

DREAM OF A GREEN CHRISTMAS

68

As December approaches, lots of kids who celebrate it start a Christmas list with their wishes for the upcoming holiday. Here's a list for a happy, eco-friendly holiday that even an eco-Scrooge could appreciate.

Buy a tree with a root bag so that you can plant it when you're done with it. Go to http://www.wikihow.com/Choose-a-Living-Christmas-Tree for more information. You may even be able to rent a live tree if you don't have anyplace to plant your tree after the holidays.

If you do get a cut tree, cut it yourself and get it at a local farm so it's not traveling a long distance to get to you. Recycle it after the holiday. Your town might have a service that will pick it up from your house and make it into mulch. Or you can go to www.earth911.org and type in your zip code to find the tree recycling service nearest you.

Use LED lights on your tree and around the house—they use less energy than the typical incandescent bulbs. Or use solar powered lights. You don't even have to plug them in!

Make your own ornaments. Glitter-covered snowflakes made from dough or cardboard never go out of style.

Make your presents instead of buying them. Everyone enjoys a creative handmade gift.

If you shop for gifts, take along your own bag instead of getting a paper or plastic one from the store.

Look for gifts with less packaging.

Make your own wrapping paper with craft paper that has a high recycled content and decorate it with stamps or stickers. Instead of tearing through the wrapping paper on your presents, pull it off gently so you can reuse it. Or try reusable gift bags. Save the ribbons and bows, too!

Save the boxes that your presents come in so that you can use them again, either for presents or another use.

The holidays are a time for many leftovers. Use yours creatively and compost the food waste.

Recycle your holiday cards by cutting and collaging them to create decorations or homemade cards for next year.

Stronger than a team of bulldozers! Able to start a worldwide movement with a single book! They're eco-heroes! Their stories can inspire you to take action, too. What is it that you care about? Endangered animals? Pollution in your local river? Global warming? Read up on your issue and the people involved in it. You'll see that anyone can go from being a concerned citizen to an eco-hero. Your eco-hero may be someone from the past or someone who is very much alive and active today. One thing's for sure—there's always room for more eco-heroes on this big planet.

ECO HEROES

RACHEL CARSON (1907-1964)
Her book *Silent Spring* (Houghton Mifflin, 1962) opened the world's eyes to the dangers of pesticides, and some say started the environmental movement.

WANGARI MAATHAI (1940-)
In 2004, she became the first African woman to receive the Nobel Peace Prize for "her contribution to sustainable development, democracy and peace." In 1977, Maathai founded the Green Belt Movement, a grassroots environmental organization, which has now planted more than 40 million trees in her native Kenya to prevent soil erosion.

MAJORA CARTER (1966-)
Don't people who live in economically depressed urban areas deserve a clean environment, too? Majora Carter has brought parks, trails, and trees to some of the poorest areas in New York City and kept garbage dumps and waste treatment plants out.

RACHEL CARSON

WANGARI MAATHAI

She's spreading the word about greening cities and making the planet healthier for everyone.

DAVID BROWER (1912-2000)

He founded several environmental organizations and stopped the damming of the Colorado River, which would have flooded part of the Grand Canyon. When critics complained that environmentalism was bad for business, he's famous for saying "No business can take place on a dead planet."

VANDANA SHIVA (1952-)

They call her the original tree-hugger. She's said to have originated the practice of hugging trees to keep them from being cut down. More than that, she's raising awareness about how corporations are using up resources in poor countries and leaving the environment contaminated.

JACQUES-YVES COUSTEAU (1910-1997)

His passion was the sea: its creatures and its life. When he saw how it was being polluted, he passionately defended it and raised awareness through his televised expeditions.

JANE GOODALL (1934-)

Protecting chimpanzees and the forests they live in has been her life's work. Inspired by her work, other animal protection groups have sprung up around the world.

MAJORA CARTER

VANDANA SHIVA

Imagine what people will be saying about you someday.

(your name and birthdate here)

_____ is known for his/her work helping/saving/creating /preserving/championing/growing/inventing (circle one or more!) _____

_____.

Here are some other heroes you can look up: Al Gore, Rebecca Aldworth, Vivian Chang, Michael Reynolds, Diane Wilson, Julia Butterfly Hill, Skye Bortoli....

70   COUNTER A SKEPTIC

SOME SAY: There's no such thing as global warming OR the planet is getting warmer, but not because of human activity.

Scientists don't all agree on what causes climate change, but the U.N. Intergovernmental Panel on Climate Change (a group of international scientists) says that it is likely (more than 90% probability) that greenhouse gases have caused most of the global warming in the past 50 years. Greenhouse gases are increased by human and industrial activity. There are over 500 studies that come to similar conclusions.
SOURCE: U.N. Panel on Climate Change

SOME SAY: Species extinctions are occurring no faster now than they were in the past.

For whatever reason, some people want to believe that everything on the planet is just fine the way it is right now. They think we should just keep doing whatever we want and not try to regulate people, or especially, businesses. Here are some of their arguments and some facts for you to use to debate with them.

Species are becoming extinct at a rate that is 100 to 1,000 times higher than it has been in recorded history. Habitat destruction and degradation of habitat are the leading causes for this phenomenon.
SOURCE: World Conservation Union

SOME SAY: It costs too much to save the environment.

Funding research for clean renewable energy sources costs much less than the subsidies and tax cuts given to oil and power companies. Protecting marine resources would cost less than current subsidies, too. SOURCE: Earth Policy Institute

SOME SAY: There is more forest in the U.S. now than there was 100 years ago.

Almost the entire continent was deforested between the late 18th and late 19th centuries. We are now starting to regain some of that. Some of the current "forests" are really tree plantations used just for logging. They're not natural habitats, and in fact, contain many invasive species. SOURCE: U.S. Forest Service

SOME SAY: Wind energy is bad because it kills birds.

In the past, the design of some wind turbines did lead to a greater-than-normal number of deaths in birds. But the designs have been improved, and now fewer birds die by running into wind turbines than die from more common causes, such as running into windows or vehicles. SOURCE: The American Wind Energy Association

SOME SAY: Greenland used to be warm in the Viking times. That proves that the Earth goes through natural periods of cold and warm.

This is a Viking-era legend. The ice caps on Greenland cover most of the island and have been there for thousands of years. SOURCE: Archives of Canada

The next time you have a conversation with a skeptic and you're not sure who's right, do some research on the topic and get back to them!

71 Think Like a Squirrel

Squirrels like to plan ahead. By the end of the summer, you can see them out there digging away, burying their nuts so that they're sure to have something good to eat in the cold of winter. Preparing for winter isn't such a bad idea for humans either. Sure, it's possible to get almost any kind of fruit or vegetable you want in the winter these days. However, those out-of-season crops travel long distances to get to you at that time of year, leaving a trail of carbon in the atmosphere as they come. If you think like a squirrel, you can have your yummy garden vegetables in the winter without the harmful emissions. How? Try canning. Despite it's name, it doesn't involve cans—it's a name for preserving food in glass jars. Jam, jelly, tomato sauce, pesto, and so many other treats—enjoy them all winter while staying clean and green.

Can it!

TOMATO SAUCE

Pick tomatoes that are ripe and unblemished.

What You'll Need (per quart jar)
1 quart (1 L) canning jar
2 tablespoons lemon juice
4 tablespoons vinegar
$1/4$-teaspoon citric acid
Pinch of salt
$3 1/2$ pounds (1.6 kg) tomatoes
Sieve
Mashing tool
Italian spices (oregano, garlic powder, onion powder)
$1/4$ cup olive oil

Wash, peel, and cut the tomatoes into chunks. Boil them in a saucepan, mashing and crushing as you add more tomatoes. When they've boiled, strain the liquid in a sieve to get out the seeds. Boil the remaining liquid, adding the lemon juice, vinegar, citric acid, and salt to acidify it. Add the oil and spices to taste.

PESTO

What You Need (per half-pint jar)
2 cups fresh basil leaves
$1/4$ cup pine nuts
$1/2$ cup olive oil
2 cloves garlic
$1/3$ cup grated fresh Parmesan cheese
Blender or food processor

Place all the ingredients in a blender or a food processor and blend until the desired consistency is achieved.

You may have been thinking about starting a collection but couldn't decide what to collect. Something important, something that will increase in value... hmmm. How about rainwater? It's completely free, has lots of uses, and provides savings for your family. Oh yeah, plants love it. To start your rainwater collection, you'll need a rain barrel. You can buy one or make your own. Position the barrel under a downspout from your roof to collect the water that runs off the roof as it rains. (Some people actually connect the barrel to the downspout.) Get a parent to drill a hole in the barrel so that you can insert a spigot for pouring. Use the water for gardening, washing the car, or cleaning things outdoors. Rainwater is the ultimate renewable resource. Don't let it go down the drain!

For more information on rain barrels and how to make them, go to www.epa.gov/region3/p2/make-rainbarrel.pdf or http://www.naturalrainwater.com/make_rainbarrel.htm.

73 Xeriscape!

It sounds like a word from an alien language. Or the name of a faraway planet. But xeriscaping (pronounced ZEE-ra-ska-ping) may be happening in your very own neighborhood right now—maybe even in your backyard. Xeriscaping is a creative way to grow a garden that doesn't use up a lot of water. Simply choose plants of a not-so-thirsty variety (see list below). Pick a drought-resistant type of grass, or cut back on grass and make more pebbled walkways or patios. Design a rock garden. Use a lot of mulch. Xeriscape gardens are great in areas experiencing drought, but no matter where you live, using less water for your garden will help conserve water. And as a bonus, you won't have to weed as much either!

Not-Too-Thirsty Plants

Artemisia
Bee balm
Black-eyed Susan
Butterfly bush
Coneflower
Daylily
Hosta
Lamb's ear
Lavender
Lantana
Stonecrop
Yarrow

74 Take Care of Yourself

Healthy you, healthy planet. How so? Local, organic food is good for your body and it's cleaner to grow and distribute. Walking or riding your bike is the clean way to travel and makes your body stronger. Plant-based products don't create toxins or carry traces of them that can get into your body or into the water, ground, or air. Bad food and exercise habits lead to bad health and the need for more health care.

Hospitals are open 24 hours a day, and they use a lot of electricity to keep all their equipment running at all times. Right now, the health care industry is the second-largest consumer of energy in the U.S. And there are many other environmental costs to health care, too, from toxic-waste disposal to the use of ozone-depleting substances. It's good to know that health care is there if you need it. But keeping yourself healthy can help make the planet healthier, too.

75 BUY THE FARM

You don't have to invest on Wall Street to become a shareholder in an important venture. Convince your parents to buy a "share" in a Community Supported Agriculture (CSA) farm. Like a share in any business, your CSA will give you a percentage of its yield, but instead of cash, it will be vegetables, fruit, or even milk, flowers, and meat. Each week during growing season, you'll get a portion of whatever grows on the farm. You can go there and pick it up yourself or go to a pick-up location. CSAs are good for the planet because they keep local food local, cutting down on all the energy needed to ship food long distances. But they're also good for your community. You get to know a farmer and the farmer gets to know her customers. CSAs aren't just for individuals. Your whole school can get its food from a local farm.

To find more about the Farm-to-School program, go to www.farmtoschool.org.

To find a CSA farm near you, go to www.localharvest.com.

76 Green What Keeps You Clean

What you put *on* your body may be just as important as what you put *in* it. Soaps, lotions, shampoo, fragrance, nail polish, and makeup all come into close, personal contact with our skin, but they aren't held to the same standards as food products. The companies that make them have ways of getting around listing all the ingredients, so you don't know *what's* in them. They can use chemicals or other ingredients that haven't been tested or even chemicals that have been proven to harm people. (The chemicals can get into the air and water during production.) Why not make your own products with natural ingredients? You'll be naturally clean, fresh, and you'll be helping the planet stay that way, too.

Stay Clean the Natural Way

With a few natural ingredients (like the ones listed below), you can make a whole bunch of different self-care products. Most of them should be available at your local natural foods store. Come up with your own recipes!

Liquid castile soap (a soap made with olive oil) * Witch hazel * Herbs—lavender, rosemary, chamomile, etc. * Herbal tea * Glycerin * Honey * Essential oils * Aloe vera juice

Natural Shampoo

Steep an herbal tea bag in boiling water (chamomile or green tea work well). Remove the tea bag. Mix equal parts water and castile soap, then pour in the tea and add a few tablespoons of olive oil. Store the mixture in a reusable container and shampoo with it. It should last about a week, depending on how many times you wash your hair.

Natural Deodorant

Mix aloe vera juice, witch hazel, and an essential oil of your choice, and pour it into a spray bottle. Use it on your feet or under your arms to get rid of odor. The ingredients will stay fresh for at least a month.

Natural Moisturizer

Mix 1 teaspoon honey, 1 teaspoon olive oil, and ¼ teaspoon lemon in a bowl. Rub it into any dry spots you may have. This mix won't keep long, so make it in small amounts and refrigerate it. You can warm it for a few seconds in the microwave before you use it.

77 Write On!

Your opinion matters! When you care about an issue and want to make a difference, write someone with the power to make a change. When you write to a decision-maker—an elected official, company board of directors, or other person in charge—you become part of the public opinion on the issue. And public opinion is always considered. When you write a letter to the editor, you can educate people on the subject. If you don't know what to say, see the opposite page for tips. A well-written letter can raise awareness, change minds, and even change the world.

How to Write a Good Letter

1. IDENTIFY YOURSELF. Tell the decision-maker or editor who you are, where you're from, and how old you are.

2. IDENTIFY YOUR PURPOSE. Explain why you're writing and why you care about this issue. Give a personal example, if you can. For example, if you're concerned about a project that will disrupt an animal's habitat, explain what the animal means to you and why you want to see it protected.

3. ASK FOR ACTION. Explain what you want the person (or organization) to do. For example, if you're writing to an elected official before a vote that will affect your issue, tell the official which way you want him or her to vote. Don't be afraid to be direct: "Please vote yes," or "Please vote no." You are a constituent (a member of the group who elected him/her) and your opinion matters. If you're writing a letter to the editor (which is, in a sense, a letter to your community), explain what you want to see happen.

4. SAY THANK YOU. Thank the decision-maker for his/her time. You can skip this part if you're writing to a newspaper.

If you're still not sure what to write, look at letters that other people have written to give you an idea about what you want to write. There are some letters you can read at http://globalresponse.org/kidsactions.php.

Who to Write

If it's a local issue, approach your city council or mayor, or write a letter to your town's paper. If the issue involves a private company, write to the board of directors. For national or international issues, write your elected representatives. You can find out who they are by going to one of these web sites and typing in your zip code.

U.S.
www.house.gov
www.senate.gov

Canada
www.parl.gc.ca

113

78 Ready? Set? Offset!

You're doing your best to make a lighter impact on our planet—recycling, consuming less, trying to use less energy. You have even calculated your carbon footprint (see page 56). But there's another tool you can use as you work to create a cleaner, greener planet—offsets. An offset is a kind of balancing tool—it helps you become more carbon neutral (see page 10). For every carbon-producing action you take, you try to take an equal, or close-to-equal carbon-reducing action. Companies do it by investing in carbon-reducing projects: building renewable energy or finding new, cleaner energy sources. You can do it yourself by planting trees, using Green Power or Green Energy options available through your local energy provider, composting, and making your house more energy efficient. If you take a car on a trip, try to walk or bike the next time. One person can make a big difference toward keeping the planet in balance.

Refrigerators and freezers help you keep food fresh longer—that's a good thing. But they also use up to $\frac{1}{6}$th of your home's energy—not so good. In fact, a refrigerator that's 10° too cold can use up to 25% more energy. You don't need Arctic temperatures to keep your food safe to eat. Set the refrigerator temperature between 35°F and 40°F (2°C and 4°C). Set the freezer control to between -5°F and 0°F (-21°C and -18°C). Keep frost from building up in your freezer—that will help it be more energy efficient (and get rid of that yucky freezer-burn taste). If your family needs to get a new fridge, get an Energy Star one—they have built-in efficiency, which is very *cool*, but not too cold.

(80) REUSE OLD NEWS

Good for the planet: recycling old newspapers. Even better for the planet: using old newspapers for art, craft, and other household projects so that you don't have to spend more money on more stuff. Try some of these ideas or come up with your own. Make it a challenge with your family—who can come up with the most creative use for old news?

PAPIER-MÂCHÉ

Papier-mâché is the ultimate earth-friendly sculpture material. All you need is some old newspapers cut into strips, flour, and water (and probably some rubber gloves to protect your hands). Mix the water and flour in a pan over low heat until it turns into a thin, glue-like substance. This is what you'll dip the newspaper strips in. What can you make with papier mâché? Picture frames, bowls, masks, baskets, puppets—the list goes on and on. Once it's dry, your papier mâché creation can be painted and no one will know that it started life as a newspaper!

SNEAKER DESTINKER

Did you know that newspapers are known for their odor-eating abilities? If you've got some stinky shoes, wad up a piece of newspaper, shove it into the toe, and let it sit overnight, or at least a few hours.

COLLAGE

Cut out words or letters in different sizes and styles and use them together with magazine pictures to make collages. A collage can be great for a school project, on a birthday card, or just as an art project.

GIFT WRAP

Presents wrapped in newspaper look really cool, especially if you use the comics section. Make sure the sheet of paper you use hasn't been crumpled up. Pick the most colorful or interesting part of the paper you can find for the top of the gift— the horoscope section or a funny headline are good choices. Use a colorful piece of ribbon, yarn, or raffia for an eye-catching contrast.

81 HOP THE BUS

Why take the bus (or subway or train or trolley) when there's a car sitting conveniently in your driveway? Because if everyone took public transportation even some of the time, the Earth would be a much cleaner place. Each car, depending on what kind it is, emits a certain amount of greenhouse gases per mile (the bigger the car, the greater the emissions). Each car taken off the road naturally reduces that amount. The more people who share a ride, the fewer harmful gases enter the atmosphere. It's that simple. There are other benefits, too. You can read or do your homework on the bus or train, it's great for people watching, and it's actually fun! Check out your local public transportation systems. Get a schedule and a transit map and figure out which routes might work for you and your parents. Cutting back on your individual car trips, even just a little, can make a big difference.

82 Shed Some Light on Watersheds

What's a watershed? Not unlike an ecosystem (see page 11), a watershed can encompass many different areas that share one feature: a common "drain"—a river, stream, lake, or even an ocean. Watersheds can tell us a lot about the health of the local environment. After a rain, all the leftover water (called run-off) pours into this drain. Run-off can come from farms that use pesticides, industrial plants that use toxic chemicals in their production, or just from the oils that accumulate on the roads and parking lots. Watersheds are home to and provide nourishment for animals and plants. And not only that—they provide our drinking water! First, find out more about your watershed (see below for a map). Then go and check it out. Do you see any signs of pollution? Become a volunteer water monitor. Start a storm drain stenciling project in your neighborhood. Your watershed needs you!

To find your watershed,
go to http://cfpub.epa.gov/surf/locate/index.cfm

To learn how you can be a volunteer water monitor, go to
www.epa.gov/owow/monitoring/volunteer/

To learn about storm drain stenciling, go to
http://dipin.kent.edu/StormDrain_Stencils.htm

83 Have A Green Halloween

What's orange, black, and green? Your next Halloween. Make your costume instead of buying a new one—why spend money on something that you're only going to wear once? You can also explore your family's wardrobe and dress-up bins for inspiration. Make your own spooky Halloween decorations from stuff you have around the house. Use soy or beeswax candles in your pumpkin—paraffin candles are made from petroleum. You could pass out organic chocolate or lollipops, or just skip sweets altogether. Give your trick-or-treaters something else, such

as stickers, seed packets, or even spare change (trick-or-treaters love that!). Carry a reusable bag, and use it again next year. Here are some more ideas for a greener Halloween:

Host a party with a contest: the best recycled costume wins!

Bubble wrap cut into strands and hung from a clear umbrella makes a great jellyfish.

Newspaper can be cut into just about anything, from a ball gown to a suit of armor.

Empty toilet paper rolls can be painted and strung together for a wacky wig.

Those old video tapes you don't watch anymore can be unwound to make a wig, too.

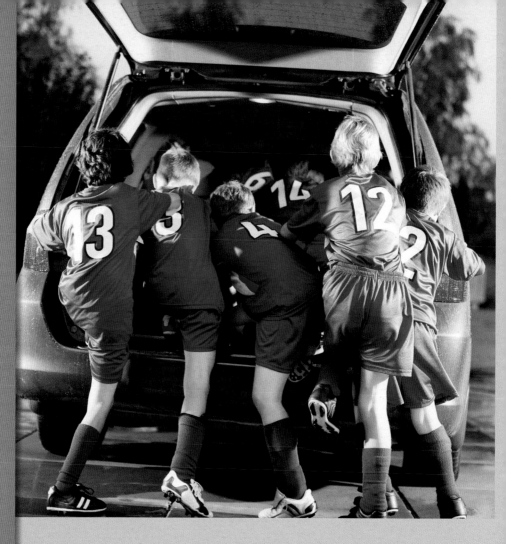

Baseball practice, scouts, or chess club: make getting there a team sport. Sharing the ride is more fun that going it alone, but it has other benefits, too. For each person who joins the trip, an additional car is taken off the road (multiply that by two if you share the ride coming and going). That adds up to a nice reduction in the amount of carbon spewing into the air and the amount of fossil fuels being used. If you share rides on a regular basis, you're really having quite an impact. Fewer cars on the road means less traffic, too. And less traffic means happier drivers. So you'll also be helping to reduce road rage!

You're getting outdoors and enjoying nature—good for you! You'll take away great memories, but make sure you also take away every trace that you were there! When camping or backpacking, make sure to take along a bag or some kind of container for your garbage, and carry it out with you when you leave. Stay on trails, not just for your own safety, but in order to protect the plants that could easily be trampled. Don't dump anything into lakes or rivers. Shampoo, soap, or other substances that are safe for you might not be for fish and other creatures that live there. If you make a campfire, use only wood that has already fallen, and make sure that it's completely extinguished before departing. Try not to make too much noise that could disturb other people or animals. If you're on the beach, don't take shells with living creatures in them. Tread lightly so that the next person who comes along can enjoy nature as much as you just did.

85 Leave Only Footprints

86 Build an Outdoor Classroom

From your seat inside your classroom, you can see the sun shining. The clouds float by and you drift into a daydream…why can't class just be outside today? How about making that dream a reality? Suggest an outdoor classroom project to your teacher. All you'll need is a place on the school grounds that's not currently being used, and permission to transform it. The spot you choose may not start out looking like much (some kids have made an outdoor classroom in a parking lot!), but if you can dream it, you can do it. Learning in your outdoor classroom is fun. But how is it good for the planet? The more "hands-on" experience you get with nature, the more you'll want to protect it. You can even apply to get money (in the form of a grant) to build your outdoor classroom! Go to www.lowes.com/community.

WHAT'S IN AN OUTDOOR CLASSROOM?

❖ Plants and garden beds
❖ Trees
❖ Seats made from tree stumps or rocks
❖ Trails
❖ A weather vane for telling the direction of the wind
❖ Bugs

❖ Snakes?!
❖ Natural light
❖ Natural art-work
❖ Water features, such as ponds
❖ A compost bin and worm habitat
❖ A temperature gauge
❖ A rainwater barrel
❖ Birds and butterflies
❖ A shed for garden tools
❖ A sundial
❖ A wooded area
❖ A climbing wall?!

WHAT'S NOT IN AN OUTDOOR CLASSROOM?

❖ A chalkboard or white board
❖ Fluorescent lights
❖ Pencil sharpeners
❖ Cubbies
❖ Hall passes

WHAT CAN YOU DO IN AN OUTDOOR CLASSROOM THAT YOU CAN'T DO INSIDE?

❖ Observe ant mounds
❖ Get dirty
❖ Get wet
❖ Feel the wind
❖ Wear a hat and gloves
❖ Run!
❖ See a new bird or bug you've never seen before
❖ Tell the time by the sun

87 Have a Green Summer

Summer is all about green! Having fun outdoors can automatically decrease your energy impact. In the summer, you have lots of opportunities to do positive things for the planet (see opposite page for ideas). Take advantage of your free schedule to do all those planet-friendly things there's not enough time for during the school year: gardening, do-it-your-self projects, or volunteering in particular. Use some of your summer reading time to make yourself more of an eco-expert (see page 26). Summer is the greenest time of the year—live easy and easy on the planet.

When the Sky Is Blue and the Grass Is Green...

- Grow your own food organically. Make dinner for your family!

- Use your rain barrel (see page 106) to water your plants. Water your grass or plants early in the day—they'll soak up more water then and it won't get wasted.

- Visit your local farmer's market and buy local food.

- Go to a PYO farm (pick your own) and gather your dinner there.

- Use reusable plates, napkins, and cutlery for your picnics.

- Turn off the computer and TV.

- Ride your bike instead of getting a ride in a car.

- Use natural insect repellents instead of chemical ones.

- Take a vacation close to home (see page 42 for more ideas).

- For outdoor cooking, use a ceramic or propane grill instead of a charcoal one. (Charcoal is a major contributor to greenhouse gases.) Or better still, cook with your solar oven (see page 34).

- Use outdoor solar lighting at night.

- Skip a few baths!

- If your area is not unbearably hot, use fans and natural breezes instead of air conditioning. If you need more cooling, make sure your home is sealed up (see page 61) and use a swamp cooler when you need it.

- Keep your curtains closed during the day so that your home stays cooler.

- Volunteer for an environmental group.

88 Let the Stars Shine

A bright streetlight on every corner can make your neighborhood safer at night. But unnecessary lighting not only wastes energy, it creates light pollution that shoots up, causing glare and "clutter" in the sky the same way garbage does on Earth. Unfocused lights make it harder for astronomers to do their job. Lights from homes at night can confuse sea turtle hatchlings, leading them toward houses instead of to the sea where they belong. Lights also obscure the constellations that migrating birds use to find their way. Check out these tips to prevent light pollution:

* Make sure outdoor lights point downward and serve a purpose: illuminating a specific path or certain area on the ground. Even better, get your parents to install light and motion sensors to outdoor lights. This way the lights will only come on when needed.
* Stand outside your home at night with your usual lights on inside. Check to make sure your lights don't "trespass" into the neighbor's property.
* Write to your local government about using sodium lamps in streetlights instead of fluorescent or incandescent light bulbs. Sodium lamps use less energy and produce less sky glow.
* While you're out at night, observe the lighting used in your area. If it's not "dark friendly" (focused on the ground and shielded), write to your city/town officials to let them know about light pollution.

For more information on light pollution and National Dark Sky Week, go to www.ndsw.org.

89 Start a Neighborhood Pool

Not the swimming kind, the sharing kind. Instead of being filled with water, it's filled with things that people have, but don't use every day. For kids, it might be sports equipment, such as a pair of ice skates, a scooter, a tent, or other camping equipment. For grownups, it might be things like tools, lawn mowers, sewing machines, juicers, or unusual kitchen appliances. The idea behind the pool is that everyone doesn't have to buy every one of those things. You can borrow and share. If there are a lot of kids in your neighborhood, why not try to organize? Figure out who has what and when they most often use it. Set up rules about respectful sharing and ways to communicate. You can create a list of shared items and a phone list, or if you or one of your parents is a techie, you could even set up your own online message board. A pool is a great way to get to know your neighbors and make sure resources don't go to waste.

90 Shhh....

Is the sound of blasting music as bad as litter on the ground? Is the noise from a leaf blower just as bad as the pollutants that it spews? Many people think so! A messy "soundscape" is not just irritating, it's bad for the Earth, too! Take a moment and just listen. What do you hear around you? The chirping of birds, or the rustling of the wind? Chances are you're just as likely to hear loud car motors, car alarms, and construction sounds. When people live together, things are going to get noisy sometimes. But the air belongs to everyone, and respecting the quiet is another way of respecting the Earth. Raking is quieter than blowing leaves, and it doesn't hurt the soundscape or the environment. Kayaks and canoes are fun on the water without the noise of motorboats or personal watercraft. You can't always control the noise others make, but you can try to live more quietly and in harmony with the Earth.

For more information on noise pollution and what you can do about it, go to www.quiet.org.

91　Please Don't Feed the Animals

A close encounter with a wild animal is an amazing experience. We all want to get a little closer and make a connection. But offering a wild animal human food isn't good for them or the environment. For animals, human food is junk food—it doesn't give them the nutrition they need and could make them sick. When animals start to see humans as a source of food, things get a little out of whack. They may stop looking for their own food sources, or they might lose their fear of humans, leading them into more populated areas where they can get hit by cars or otherwise injured. If they become accustomed to getting food in a certain place, they might become aggressive if the food isn't there. You eat your food, they eat theirs—just the way nature intended.

92 Love Your Mother

In ancient Greece she was *Gaia*; in Rome she was *Terra*. To the Celts, she was *Danu*; and to the Inca she was *Pachamama*. Throughout time, our ancestors have had many different names for Mother Earth, but their beliefs about her have been surprisingly similar: she provides us with life, nourishment, and shelter, and all living things are part of her. Because they saw the Earth as a mother, the ancients respected her and all her creatures like family members. Native Americans called the wind, the sun, and the moon their brothers and sisters. Those old beliefs have something to teach us. We're in a close personal relationship with the planet, and we need to treat it like family. If everyone did a little more giving and a little less taking, we'd be a much happier family.

EARTH FAMILY CHORES

✔ Take out the recycling
✔ Make bed (in the garden)
✔ Clean outdoor room
✔ Wash clothes (in cold water)
✔ Hang clothes to dry (outside, to save energy)

93 Take the 1-Mile Challenge

It's not a race: it's a choice. If you have somewhere to go—school, the park, the library, a friend's house—and you know it's less than a mile away, walk, bike, or skate there instead of asking your parents for a ride. Or walk one way, and get a lift back. A mile is only 5,280 feet or 1,760 yards (1.6 km). While the fastest athletes in the world may be able to run a mile in 5 minutes, you'll be able to walk one in 20 minutes or so. And if you speed walk, you could probably make it in 15. For every mile you walk, you'll be keeping about 1 pound of carbon emissions out of the atmosphere, and you'll be getting in better shape. Perhaps there's a 5-minute mile in your future!

Giving your time to an environmental organization may just be the best thing you can do for yourself *and* the planet. Here's why. Since groups that help the Earth are *nonprofits* (meaning they're not in the business of making money), they often can't pay people to do jobs that need doing. The jobs could be really small, such as stuffing envelopes, or bigger, such as helping feed animals. But big or small, they're important, and often they're jobs that kids can do! Find a cause that's important to you (animals, organic food, clean air, pollution) and an organization that supports it. Chances are there's a group in your area that's working on that very issue, and you can help them. Good for the planet, but how is it good for you? You get real work experience before you're old enough to work, and you'll learn a lot about the cause that's important to you.

94 VOLUNTEER!

To find volunteer opportunities in your area try www.idealist.org or www.volunteermatch.org.

95 Lose the Labels

The Earth belongs to all of us, and many people feel passionately about what's right and wrong for it. Conversations about the environment can get pretty heated when people have different opinions. But name calling and labels won't get anybody anywhere. The only way to make progress on environmental issues is to work together and try to find common ground. When you talk about your feelings and opinions on an issue, try not to blame or call names. Instead, focus on the benefits that a healthy environment holds for everyone. If you set a positive tone, it's likely that others will follow. Before you know it, you might have convinced others to see your point of view. It's a win-win situation for you and the planet.

BEE HELPFUL

96

Learn more about honeybees and all they do. Check out these websites:
www.thehoneybeeproject.com
www.helpthehoneybees.com

No matter how small, each creature in our worldwide ecosystem plays an important role in keeping our planet going. Take honeybees, for example—those little winged creatures are responsible for pollinating millions of plants that we need for food. But in recent years they've been dying in huge numbers: Some scientists even say wild honeybees could become extinct before you graduate from high school! No one knows exactly what the cause is, but there are some things you can do to help:

If you see a swarm of honeybees, don't spray it—bees swarm gently unless they're disturbed. Instead, contact your local nature center to see if they can put you in touch with a beekeeper who can take the swarm away and protect it.

Plant bee-friendly plants in your garden. With more bees, your fruit and vegetable plants will thrive, and the bees will, too.

Eat local honey! That will keep honeybees strong in your area.

Write to your elected officials. Let them know that endangered honeybees affect local farmers, and ask them to fund research to help solve the problem.

Become a Garbage Inspector

Roll up your sleeves and put on the rubber gloves—it's time to start digging through the garbage. Doing a trash audit can help your family use your resources more wisely. Here's what to do:

◆ Start on a Sunday or Monday with an empty garbage bag. When it's full, weigh it. Record the weight. Go outside and lay a tarp down. Dump the contents of the bag onto the tarp.

◆ Sort through the garbage identifying categories: food waste, paper, plastic, etc. Separate the trash into piles. Note which is biggest. Write down all your findings.

◆ Continue this process throughout the week. Then call a family meeting to report in. Together, figure out what you could be recycling or how you could cut back. Could you compost the food waste? Recycle more paper? Buy in bulk?

◆ Once you've made your decisions, repeat your audit, making sure you weigh the garbage again. Did your garbage decrease? If so, congratulate yourselves! If not, have another family meeting to figure out how you can improve.

TIPS FOR TRASH

◆ Print out a sign for the lid of your garbage bin: HEY YOU! Can you recycle that?

◆ Place recycle bins right next to your trash to make it easy to remember.

◆ Place a compost bin next to your trash to make it easy to think about composting food waste.

If your family trash audit goes well, why not do one at your school? It's a great activity for an eco-club, or just for a class project.

98 See How Low You Can Go

As winter approaches, lower the thermostat 1° for a week. Once you're used to that temperature, lower it another degree. See how low you can go. And when summer comes around, see how long you can go without the air conditioner. If you have to turn it on, see how high you can keep the thermostat!

Peel Them Off or Pile Them On

Layering your clothes is the easiest way to achieve personal temperature control and be more energy efficient, too. When you're feeling a chill, reach for a sweater or blanket and warm socks instead of the thermostat. If you're starting to break a sweat, peel off some layers and get yourself a cool drink. Keeping your thermostat even 1° lower in the winter and higher in the summer reduces your carbon output and saves up to 3% of your home energy cost. And if you made a 2° adjustment, you could prevent as much as 2,000 pounds (910 kg) of carbon from entering the atmosphere. (That's like taking a cross-country-bound car off the road). Who knew a sweater could be so powerful?

Even with your eyes closed you can tell when there's a school bus running nearby. That deep throttling sound the engine makes, that certain smell in the air. Almost all school buses run on diesel, a kind of fuel that's often used for larger, noisy engines. The smell comes from exhaust fumes exiting the bus's tailpipe, and those fumes are full of toxic chemicals such as benzene. Diesel tailpipe emissions aren't just bad for the air; they're bad for your health. They can be especially harmful when the bus is idling—when the engine is running, but the bus isn't moving, such as when bus drivers are waiting to pick up kids. Find out if your school district has an anti-idling rule or if the buses have been fitted with new equipment that cleans the emissions. If not, you have a project for your environmental club or science class. Harmful bus emissions affect kids more than anyone—kids are the best ones to help stop them.

NO
PARKED
IDLING
$500 FINE
BY ORDER OF
METROPOLITAN
POLICE DEPARTMENT

For more
information,
check out:
http://epa.gov/clean
schoolbus/antiidling.htm

100 TUNE IN

In the old days, sailors could navigate by the stars. Farmers knew when to plant their crops by watching when the leaves unfurled on the trees. Nature has so much to tell us—if we just listen. Animals and plants are usually the first ones to let us know if there's something harmful in the air or water. (Consider the canary in the coalmine: If the bird died, there was harmful methane in the air and miners had to get out.) Tune in to nature. Are there fewer birds in your yard this year than last? Fewer fish in your local lake? Is it warmer than usual in spring this year? Has the summer been drier or wetter than it normally is? Note your observations, and see if you can get answers. Listening to nature is the first step to understanding our planet's health.

101 Don't Stop Here

You've ticked everything off your list. Congratulations! But don't stop here. A planet protector's work is never done! A list—even as long as the one in this book—can never really be complete. There will always be new ways for you contribute in your own special ways—ways no one may have ever even thought of before. Keep your eyes open and stay in tune with the world around you. Figure out what's important to you and take action! When grownups say "the future belongs to you," it's more than just a bunch of words. You *can* change the world and make it a better place. The great peace activist Mahatma Gandhi said, "Be the change you want to see in the world." Carry those words with you, and there's no doubt that you'll make a difference.

Sources

I included a lot of facts in this book. Here's where I got my information.

Page 15

17 million barrels of oil are used each year to produce all the disposable plastic water bottles used in the U.S.: Pacific Institute, http://www.pacinst.org/. "Bottled Water and Energy: Getting to 17 Million Barrels." December 2007.

Only about 12 percent of disposable water bottles are recycled.: "Plastic Bottles Pile Up As Mountains of Waste." Miguel Llanos. MSNBC: March 3, 2005.

Page 19

…each person in North America will receive more than 500 pieces of junk mail this year.: Based on calculations from The U.S. Postal Service

To make those throw-away catalogs and letters, each year, it takes 100 million trees.: New American Dream calculation from Conservatree and U.S. Forest Service statistics/ http://www.newdream.org/junkmail/facts.php

Page 25

…water heating is third-largest expense in your monthly bill.: The U.S. Department of Energy

Page 27

If you reduce your margins to .75, studies show you'll save 4.75% paper.: The Penn State Green Destiny Council

Page 29

…if it's organic, there's minimal risk of harmful chemicals getting into you through your food.: University of Washington study

Page 32

…each year around 30 million trees are used to make books sold in the United States alone.: The Green Press Initiative

Page 36

Some studies show that each kid more or less throws away his or her weight in lunch garbage every year.: Wastefreelunches.org

Page 37

Each mile driven in an average car contributes close to a pound of CO_2 to the atmosphere.: Barbara Hirsch. "49 Short Eco Facts." UCSB Sustainability (University of California Santa Barbara Sustainability: March 2007.

Page 38

…kids who study by natural light actually get better grades.: Natural Resources Defense Council

Page 48

All facts come from The U.S. Environmental Protection Agency and Environment Canada

Page 56

Packaging accounts for more than half the paper produced in the U.S. and almost half of it ends up un-recycled, in landfills.: The Dogwood Alliance

Page 58

…strong chemical cleaners do the job, they usually have side effects. They can cause allergies, trigger asthma attacks…: The U.S. National Center for Health Statistics

…and can release toxins into the air, ground, or water.: US Geological Survey Report, 2002

Page 61

Air leaking out through windows and under doors can make homes up to 30 percent less energy efficient.: The U.S. Department of Energy

Page 62

…the fuel used to make a single hamburger is equal to driving 20 miles in a car.: www.peta.com

Page 63

Every time you run the washing machine, around 41 gallons of water go down the drain.: The U.S. Environmental Protection Agency

Page 64

If everyone in the U.S. switched just one old bulb to compact fluorescent, it would be like taking 800,000 cars

off the road, and enough energy would be saved to power 3 million homes for a year! : The U.S. Department of Energy

Page 66

In time, they'll eat their body weight in food each day…: "Worms as Environmental Saviors?" Rachel Oliver. CNN: October 2, 2007.

Page 69

Each individual in the U.S. and Canada produces an average of 4.6 pounds of garbage per day, contributing to a total of more than 251 tons of annual garbage, 34 percent of which is paper…: The U.S. Environmental Protection Agency and Environment Canada

Page 70

…an average bat is said to be able to eat up to 300 insects a night!: The Bat Conservation Trust

Page 81

1 tree = 700 grocery bags.: The California Energy Commission

Both paper and plastic bags can be recycled, but only 10 to 15% of paper bags and 1 to 3% of plastic bags are being recycled.: The Wall Street Journal

It takes more than four times as much energy to manufacture a paper bag as it does to manufacture a plastic bag.: 1989 Plastic Recycling Directory, Society of Plastics Industry

Plastic bags create four times as much solid waste… To make all the bags we use each year, it takes 14 million trees for paper and 12 million barrels of oil for plastic…Since plastic is cheaper to produce, most stores use them. The average family uses nearly 1,500 plastic bags per year.: reusablebags.com

Page 84

On average, Americans use the most paper each year: 650 pounds of paper each year, which uses up more than 4 billion trees a year.: The Clean Air Council

Page 86

Two glasses of water are used to clean each glass of water brought to your table at a restaurant.: The City of San Diego Water Department

The rest of the facts in this entry come from The U.S. Environmental Protection Agency.

Page 95

All facts come from Conservation International.

Page 108

Right now, the health care industry is the second-largest consumer of energy in the U.S.: The U.S. Department of Energy

Page 110

All facts come from the Environmental Working Group.

Page 115

But they also use up to $1/6^{th}$ of your home's energy… a refrigerator that's 10 degrees too cold can use up to 25% more energy.: The California Energy Commission

Page 126

Lights also obscure the constellations that migrating birds use to find their way.: International Dark Sky Association

Page 131

For every mile you walk, you'll be keeping about 1 pound of carbon emissions out of the atmosphere.: The U.S. Environmental Protection Agency

Page 134

Some scientists even say wild honeybees could become extinct before you graduate from high school.: calculation based on facts gathered from http://www.thehoneybeeproject.com/thebees.html

Page 136

Keeping your thermostat even 1 degree lower in the winter and higher in the summer reduces your carbon output and saves up to 3% of your home energy cost. And if you made a 2 degree adjustment, you could prevent as much as 2,000 pounds of carbon from entering the atmosphere.: The Rocky Mountain Institute

Photo Credits

Page 5: clockwise from top left: © Manfred Steinbach/Shutterstock Inc.; © Elena Elisseeva/Shutterstock Inc.; © Ilyas Kalimullin/Shutterstock Inc.; © Gary Paul Lewis/Shutterstock Inc.; © toriru/Shutterstock Inc.; © prism_68/Shutterstock Inc.; (bees) © Vinicius Tupinamba/Shutterstock Inc.

Page 6: (boy) © Gabe Palmer/zefa/Corbis; (field) © Serg64/Shutterstock Inc.

Page 8: © Serghei Starus/Shutterstock Inc.

Page 9: (top) © Carmen Martínez Banús/IStockphoto.com; (bottom) © Muellek/Shutterstock Inc.

Page 10: © Nagy Melinda/Shutterstock Inc.

Page 11: © Joe Gough/Shutterstock Inc.

Page 12: © Sarah Cates/IStockphoto.com

Page 13: © Michael Mihin/Shutterstock Inc.

Page 14: (top) © Chris Harvey/Shutterstock Inc.; (bottom) © Achim Prill/IStockphoto.com

Page 15: (top) © prism_68/Shutterstock Inc.; (bottom) © Péter Gudella/Shutterstock Inc.

Page 16: © sonya etchison/Shutterstock Inc.; (illustration) © ZTS/Shutterstock Inc.

Page 17: (cat) © Dwight Smith/IStockphoto.com; (toy) © Shutterstock Inc.; (rabbit) © Regien Paassen/Shutterstock Inc.

Page 18: (top) © Charles F McCarthy/Shutterstock Inc.; (bottom) © Kirk Peart Professional Imaging/Shutterstock Inc.

Page 19: (trees) © Anders Aagesen/IStockphoto.com;

(mail) © Kenneth C. Zirkel/IStockphoto.com

Page 20: © Monkey Business Images/Shutterstock Inc.; (bubbles) © buzya kalapkina/Shutterstock Inc.

Page 22: © Galina Barskaya/Shutterstock Inc.

Page 23: (crayons) © Douglas Freer/Shutterstock Inc.; (shoes) © Timothy Large/Shutterstock Inc.; (pen) © bluestocking/IStockphoto.com

Page 24: © Galina Barskaya/Shutterstock Inc.

Page 25: (top) © Marie-france Bélanger/IStockphoto.com; (bottom) © Carmen Martínez Banús/IStockphoto.com

Page 26: © Imagesource/MediaBakery

Page 28: © Sascha Burkard/Shutterstock Inc.

Page 29: © Atlantide Phototravel/Corbis

Page 30: (calendar) © OnlyVectors/Shutterstock Inc.; © Mikko Pitkänen/Shutterstock Inc.

Page 31: (cranes) © Joel Bauchat Grant/Shutterstock Inc.; (fish) © frantisekhojdysz/Shutterstock Inc.; (mountains) © Christoph63/Shutterstock Inc.

Page 32: © Carmen Martínez Banús/IStockphoto.com

Page 33: © Anastasiya Igolkina/Shutterstock Inc.

Pages 34-35: © Lark Books

Page 36: (top) © Gary Cookson/Shutterstock Inc.; (bottom) © Lorraine Kourafas/Shutterstock Inc.

Page 37: (top) logo used courtesy of http://www.iwalktoschool.org.; (bottom) © Design Pics/MediaBakery

Page 38: © PHOTOCREO Michal Bednarek/Shutterstock Inc.

Page 39: © Monkey Business Images/Shutterstock Inc.;

(hamburger) © kotik1/Shutterstock Inc.

Page 40: © image100/MediaBakery

Page 41: (top) © PhotoSky 4t com/Shutterstock Inc.; (bottom) © Thomas Barrat/Shutterstock Inc.

Page 42: © Marilyn Nieves/IStockphoto.com

Page 43: © Glenda Powers/IStockphoto.com; (background design) © Steven Bourelle/Shutterstock Inc.

Page 44: © Digital Vision/MediaBakery

Page 45: © Chen Ping Hung/Shutterstock Inc.

Page 46: © Photo and logo used courtesy of The Southern Energy & Environment Expo

Page 48: (top) © Stefan Redel/Shutterstock Inc.; (bottom) © Dole/Shutterstock Inc.

Page 49: (flower) © Dole/Shutterstock Inc.; (girl) © Ivonne Wierink/Shutterstock Inc.

Page 50: © Mana Photo/Shutterstock Inc.

Page 51: (batteries) © objectsforall/Shutterstock Inc.; (boy) © Monkey Business Images/Shutterstock Inc.

Page 52: © Corbis/MediaBakery

Page 53: © Jani Bryson/IStockphoto.com

Page 54: © Corbis/MediaBakery

Page 55: (boots) © Jennifer Photography & Imaging/IStockphoto.com; (footprints) © Daniel Cooper/IStockphoto.com

Page 56: (boxes) © Peter Hansen/Shutterstock Inc.; (CDs) © Pablo Eder/Shutterstock Inc.

Page 57: © Radu Razvan/Shutterstock Inc.

Page 58: © Guryanov Oleg/Shutterstock Inc.

Page 59: © Vasca/Shutterstock Inc.; (lemons) Valentyn Volkov/Shutterstock Inc.

Page 60: (top) © Imagesource/MediaBakery; (bottom) image courtesy of KidStuff Public Relations and Matter Group, LLC

Page 61: © Svetlana Larina/Shutterstock Inc.

Page 62: (top) © Blend Images/MediaBakery; (bottom) © Denis Pepin/Shutterstock Inc.

Page 63: © image100/MediaBakery

Page 64: (top) © Zoran Vukmanov Simokov/Shutterstock Inc.; (bottom) © Maciej Korzekwa/IStockphoto.com

Page 65: (background) © Jan Martin Will/Shutterstock Inc.; (kids) © Corbis/MediaBakery

Page 66: (top) © Lisa Fletcher/IStockphoto.com; (bottom) © Dusty Cline/Shutterstock Inc.

Page 67: © Lisa Fletcher/IStockphoto.com

Page 68: (notebook) © Curt Ziegler/Shutterstock Inc.; (pencils) © 6493866629/Shutterstock Inc.

Page 69: © Gorich/Shutterstock Inc.

Page 70: (top) © Alexei Zaycev/IStockphoto.com; (bottom) © Nicholas Rjabow/Shutterstock Inc.

Page 71: © Jerome Whittingham/Shutterstock Inc.

Pages 72-73: © Lark Books

Page 74: © Schmid Christophe/Shutterstock Inc.

Page 75: © Matsonashvili Mikhail/Shutterstock Inc.

Page 76: © guentermanaus/Shutterstock Inc.

Page 77: (top) © Manfred Steinbach/Shutterstock Inc.; (bottom) Yasonya/Shutterstock Inc.

Page 78: © Elena Elisseeva/Shutterstock Inc.

Page 79: © Digital Vision/MediaBakery

Page 80: © Christy Thompson/ Shutterstock Inc.

Page 81: © Lim Yong Hian/Shutterstock Inc.

Page 82: © Thomas M. Perkins/ Shutterstock Inc.

Page 83: © Imagesource/MediaBakery

Page 84: © Michael D. Brown/ Shutterstock Inc.

Page 85: (mug) © Marek Szumlas/ Shutterstock Inc.; (honeycomb) © matzsoca/ Shutterstock Inc.; (cartridge) © Alex Melnick/Shutterstock Inc.; (chocolate) © Norman Pogson/Shutterstock Inc.

Page 86: (background) © Chepko Danil Vitalevich/ Shutterstock Inc.; (faucet) © Simon Voorwinde/Shutterstock Inc.

Page 87: (top) © Denisenko/ Shutterstock Inc.; (bottom) © suemack/IStockphoto.com

Page 88: (background) © gualtiero boffi/Shutterstock Inc.; (boys) © Digital Vision/ MediaBakery

Page 89: (background) © Marilyn Volan/Shutterstock Inc.; (caterpillar) © Leigh Prather/ Shutterstock Inc.; (rabbits) © Joshua Lewis/Shutterstock Inc.; (trees) © Christopher Elwell/Shutterstock Inc.; (squirrel) © Eric Isselée/ Shutterstock Inc.; (bird) © Al Mueller/Shutterstock Inc.

Page 90: © toriru/Shutterstock Inc.; (glasses) © Anke van Wyk/Shutterstock Inc.

Page 91: (top) © Jaimie D. Travis/ IStockphoto.com; (bottom) © KK Art & Photography/Shutterstock Inc.

Page 92: (map) © Rafa Irusta/ Shutterstock Inc.; (stamp) © argus/Shutterstock Inc.; (barcode) © Feng Yu/Shutterstock Inc.

Page 93: © JLP/Jose L. Pelaez/ Corbis

Page 94: (background) © Velychko/Shutterstock Inc.; (canoe) © Georgy Markov/ Shutterstock Inc.

Page 95: (forest) © Brasil2/IStockphoto.com; (orangutans) © George Clerk/IStockphoto.com

Page 96: (top) © Greg Gardner/ IStockphoto.com; (bottom) © Vladimir Popovic/Shutterstock Inc.

Page 97: © Oleg Kozlov, Sophy Kozlova/Shutterstock Inc.

Page 98: © Lori Sparkia/Shutterstock Inc.

Page 99: © Tereza Dvorak/Shutterstock Inc.

Pages 100-101: Image of Rachel Carson courtesy of U.S. Fish & Wildlife Service; (Wangari Maathai) © Wanjira Mathia ; (Majora Carter) © James Burling Chase ; (Vandana Shiva) courtesy of

Page 102: © laurent hamels/ Shutterstock Inc.

Page 103: © Rafa Irusta/Shutterstock Inc.

Page 104: © Ilyas Kalimullin/ Shutterstock Inc.

Page 105: (top) © Dale Wagler/ Shutterstock Inc.; (bottom) © matka_Wariatka/Shutterstock Inc.

Page 106: (top) © David Cannings-Bushell/IStockphoto.com; (bottom) © Imagine/ Shutterstock Inc.

Page 107: © Ginger Graziano (Image used courtesy of Ginger Graziano)

Page 108: © Gary Paul Lewis/ Shutterstock Inc.

Page 109: © Noam Armonn/ Shutterstock Inc.

Pages 110-111: © Lark Books

Page 112: (top) © Arvind Balaraman/Shutterstock Inc.; (bottom) © Darko Novakovic/ Shutterstock Inc.

Page 113: (top) © Monkey Business Images/Shutterstock Inc.; (bottom) © Tatiana Mironenko/Shutterstock Inc.

Page 114: (top) © Vincent Voigt/ IStockphoto.com; (bottom) © Sharon Day/IStockphoto.com

Page 115: © UpperCut/MediaBakery

Page 116: © OJO Images/MediaBakery

Page 117: © Blend Images/MediaBakery

Page 118: © Xavier MARCHANT/ Shutterstock Inc.

Page 119: (left) © Liza McCorkle/ IStockphoto.com; (right) © Tammy Bryngelson/IStockphoto.com

Page 120: © Corbis/MediaBakery

Page 121: © Noam Armonn/ Shutterstock Inc.

Page 122: (top) © UpperCut/ MediaBakery; (bottom) © Kshishtof/Shutterstock Inc.

Page 123: (ladybug) © Tomasz Pietryszek/Shutterstock Inc.; (moth) © Potapov Alexander/ Shutterstock Inc.; (bird) © Eric Isselée/Shutterstock Inc.; (background) © Ant Clausen/ Shutterstock Inc.

Page 124: © Jacek Chabraszewski/Shutterstock Inc.

Page 125: © Elena Elisseeva/ Shutterstock Inc.

Page 126: (background) © zphoto/Shutterstock Inc.; (parking lot) © prism_68/ Shutterstock Inc.

Page 127: (bike) © Gravicapa/ Shutterstock Inc.; (ladder) © Perov Stanislav/Shutterstock Inc.; (lawn mower) © Simon Krzic/Shutterstock Inc.; (tent) © ene/Shutterstock Inc.

Page 128: (background) © Vinka/ Shutterstock Inc.; (girl) © Courtnee Mulroy/Shutterstock Inc.

Page 129: © Sergey Karpov/ Shutterstock Inc.

Page 130: © Lark Books

Page 131: © Jon Feingersh/ Corbis

Page 132: © Valerie Loiseleux/ IStockphoto.com

Page 133: © Jacek Chabraszewski/IStockphoto.com

Page 134: © Vinicius Tupinamba/ Shutterstock Inc.

Page 135: © Corbis/MediaBakery

Page 136: (top) © Miles Boyer/ Shutterstock Inc.; (bottom) © GoodMood Photo/Shutterstock Inc.

Page 137: (sign) © Stephen Finn/ Shutterstock Inc.; (buses) © Glen Jones/Shutterstock Inc.

Page 138: © Blend Images/MediaBakery

Page 139: © Corbis/MediaBakery